Bench Marks of Faith

by

Ewart G. Watts

Study Aids

by

John P. Gilbert

D1198445

tidings

1908 Grand Avenue
Nashville, Tennessee 37203

CONTENTS

INTRODUCTION

Near the end of his career, Victor Hugo, the great French novelist, wrote, "For half a century I have been writing my thoughts in prose and verse; but I feel that I have not said one-thousandth part of what is in me."

I have not been writing for half a century, but I have been writing and speaking for thirty-three years. Sunday after Sunday, week-in-and-week-out, as a local pastor I have been writing and speaking my understanding of the good news God has given in Jesus Christ. Half of that time has been with one congregation. So, I must confess there have been times when it seemed I had said everything I felt or believed about this gospel. In my sixteen year pastorate, I wrote and preached at least 1,800,000 words—the equivalent of twenty-eight, two hundred page books. So there have been almost desperate times when I asked myself, "How else can I say it? I have already said it in every way I know or can imagine. They are bound to be tired of hearing me say it." On the other hand, there have been times when I have felt as Victor Hugo said he did—that I have not said one-thousandth part of what I feel and know about what Paul called "the depth of the riches and wisdom and knowledge of God." (Romans 11:33, NEB.) It is like trying to exhaust an ever-flowing artesian well or struggling to empty the Pacific Ocean with a bucket.

As the call came to move from the local pastorate to

another field of witness, I felt it would be of great help to me personally and perhaps of some help to the members of my congregation, to try to bring together and articulate what I believed to be the most important and essential points of the gospel I had been trying to proclaim. So, during Lent and Easter I preached the sermons which have now been expanded into the chapters of this book.

While they come out of my own life and Christian experience, they are greatly influenced by the congregation where they were preached. Most of what is said here was written as pastor and people sought to minister to each other through the joys and sorrows, the births and the deaths, the confirmations and weddings, the study groups and the counseling sessions, and all the other associations and experiences which join pastor and people together in the church life. There is a very real sense in which the members of First United Methodist Church, Topeka, Kansas have joined in writing this book.

There is no attempt here to present a comprehensive summary of the Christian faith. This has already been done by any number of great theologians. All that is attempted here is to single out and illustrate some of the important truths which I have tried to emphasize in my preaching, and which I believe will stand the test of time.

A new and important element has been added to these sermons in the "Suggestions For Group Study." They have been written by the Rev. John P. Gilbert, Associate Editor of Adult Church School Publications. I am most grateful for this contribution. They provide the "talk back" dimension which is so important in keeping the reader from being brain-washed by the author.

INTRODUCTION FOR STUDY GROUPS

Bench Marks of Faith can be an exciting study resource for a group of persons seeking to understand their own faith more completely. Use this series of sermons in any study setting—Sunday morning church school, perhaps one evening each week during Lent, a churchwide weekend retreat, or simply several couples who want to gather to study and to grow together.

Six to fifteeen persons make up a good study group; try to include in your group persons with different ideas and viewpoints. You'll find a study group of youth and adults together especially exciting. Agree together as members of the study group to attend sessions regularly, to read in advance assigned portions of this book, and to participate honestly and openly in the sessions.

The suggestions for group study that follow each of the chapters in this book provide some ideas for studying each of the sermons. These suggestions are written so the group can "lead itself." You'll want to designate a leader for each of the sessions, but don't expect this leader to be an "authority with all the answers."

And regularly share ideas, experiences, and opinions of your own bench marks of faith, for this sharing is central to any learning experience.

Commence your study of each of these sermons by clarifying your understanding of exactly what the writer is saying. Here are several ways you might do this:

1. Open each session by inviting questions or comments for clarification of the sermon. Questions such as, "What new idea in this sermon excited you?" "With what points in this sermon do you disagree?" or "What was the writer's main idea in this sermon?" might help start such a period of discussion.

2. Ask one or several persons to come to a session prepared to outline the sermon on chalkboard or newsprint. This outline should be fairly detailed and extensive, focusing on the writer's main ideas.

3. Work as a whole group in outlining the sermon by going through the sermon paragraph by paragraph, listing on chalkboard or newsprint the main idea of each paragraph.

4. Chapters in this book are sermons. From time to time ask a group member to come prepared to read a chapter as a sermon, providing vocal inflection, gestures, and other public speaking techniques. When he or she has finished, allow the rest of the group to ask questions of the "preacher": "What did you mean by this statement?" or "Describe your idea about that point more completely."

I

A FATHERLY LOVE IS IN CHARGE

"The God who created the world and everything in it, and who is Lord of heaven and earth, does not live in shrines made by men." (Acts 17:24, NEB.)

The words printed above are from Paul's speech to some of the leading citizens of Athens. On first reading, they may not seem to have much of a modern application. They were addressed to some pagans who had erected all sorts of stone monuments and shrines to a whole pantheon of gods. Our first reaction may be to exclaim, "This doesn't apply to us. We don't worship stone idols anymore." But, neither did those to whom Paul was speaking.

These words were not addressed to illiterate barbarians who were worshiping stone idols. Paul was talking to men who were disciples of Socrates and Plato—men who prided themselves on being able to understand and define everything. That was their trouble. Through their logic and their philosophy, they assumed they knew all about divinity. They knew what the gods were up to and exactly what men should do to get along with them. But, Paul was challenging this assumption that God can be housed in man made shrines, confined to man made definitions, limited by human knowledge.

I believe he would throw out a similar challenge today to some of our theologians and philosophers who feel they have God all figured out. They have whittled him down to

human dimensions and human terms so we can all understand him. They have been so intent on proving that God
is no longer "out there" or "up there" that they have just
about ruled out any supernatural or transcendental element altogether. In effect they say, "We refuse to accept
any reality which cannot be explained by our experience
and our logic." One perceptive interpreter of our time
writes, "We are . . . in a situation in which transcendence
has been reduced to a rumor." [1] Another writes, "We have
sort of a general anaesthesia of our sense of the Holy, a
numbing of our awareness of Encompassing Mystery." [2]

The first of these comments was not written by a
preacher. It was written by Peter Berger, a sociologist
who has been very critical of the other-worldliness of the
church. He wrote a book entitled THE NOISE OF SOLEMN
ASSEMBLIES in which he accused the Church of being
more concerned with maintaining its rituals and forms
than working for justice and righteousness in society. But
now, in a book entitled A RUMOR OF ANGELS, he says,
in effect, perhaps we have been wrong in ruling out a
transcendent or supernatural element, in pretending that
everything depends on what man can understand and do.
He suggests that we can become such dogmatic humanists
that we fail to hear or see the clear signals of transcendence which might keep us from missing the boat. He
insists that there must be a new openness in our perception of reality which is willing to recognize that there is
more than just a human dimension to life. He concludes,
"To reaffirm this discovery of God in our situation might
necessitate the formulation of new creeds, though their
content would in this case be quite traditional—the reaffirmation of God who is not the world and who was not
made by man, who is outside and not within ourselves,
who is not a sign of human things but of whom human
things are signs, who is symbolized and not a symbol.
It is this God, totally other and yet accessible in human
experience, in whom faith will see the foundation of order,
justice, and compassion in the world." [3]

Did you notice how much this speech by a secular sociologist sounds like Paul's speech on Mars hill in Athens?

Berger calls for a "reaffirmation of a God who is not the world and who was not made by men." Paul spoke of a God who is Lord of heaven and earth, and who does not live in shrines made by men.

Does this mean that this sociologist has stopped being scientific and started being sentimental? Has he stopped being a hard-headed scientist? No, he would say that having a closed mind and refusing to see evidence of a power and a purpose beyond the mind and the power of human-kind is as unscientific as the theologian who refuses to see or accept the facts discovered by science.

It's interesting to note that Dr. Alfred Whitehead who is considered to be the philosopher of modern science also affirms the reality and importance of something beyond the finite understanding of man. He wrote, "Religion is the vision of something which stands beyond, behind, and within, the passing flux of immediate things; something which is real, and yet waiting to be realized; something which is a remote possibility, and yet the greatest of present facts; something that gives meaning to all that passes, and yet eludes apprehension; something whose possession is the final good, and yet is beyond all reach; something which is the ultimate ideal, and the hopeless quest." [4]

But, you say, isn't this an other-worldliness which lets us off the hook and makes us look for supernatural solutions when we need to roll up our sleeves and work to build a better world where we are? If we start being concerned about something "which stands beyond and behind . . . the passing flux of immediate things" don't we lose a real sense of urgency about reforming and building a better world?

Of course, as a sociologist, Peter Berger is very much concerned about such reforms, so he replies: "This in no way implies a remoteness from the moral challenges of the moment, but rather the most careful attention to each human gesture that we encounter or that we may be called upon to perform in the everyday dramas of human life . . . just because, in the words of the New Testament . . . it is in the midst of these affairs that 'some have entertained

angels unawares.' " [5] In other words, the very fact that the
Creator is best known and understood through those he
creates and supports, makes us that much more concerned
about their welfare. As he said before, "it is this God,
totally other and yet accessible in human experience, in
whom faith will see the foundation of order, justice, and
compassion in the world." This means that if men believe
that the building of a good society, with justice and lib-
erty for all, is part of a Divine plan and purpose, they are
much more likely to sacrifice and work for it than they are
if such a society is nothing but a man-made dream. It
makes a big difference whether your ultimate loyalty is
to a "Kingdom of God" or a "Kingdom of Man." When
Jesus called men to seek first the Kingdom of God, he was
emphasizing the most important element in the fight for
social reform.

For one thing, if this element is missing, we are confronted by the grave danger which is illustrated by atheis-
tic Communism or pagan Naziism. And when you put the
tools of modern science in the hands of either, the danger
is compounded and magnified. Unless man feels a solemn
obligation to some just power beyond himself, he is sure
to destroy himself and his civilization. All the great historians have emphasized this fact. All the great Biblical
prophets have affirmed it. A disintegrating society is a
society that worships itself and concentrates entirely upon
the values which it knows. It sees no other values as
transcending them or standing in judgment over them. In
Paul's words, it tries to keep its God confined in "shrines
made by men."

Of course, we are quick to spot this danger in a Communist Russia or a Nazi Germany, but what about the
danger in our own country? Isn't there the same danger
here if we blandly assume that God is always on our side,
that the American way is his way?

I think it is clear that firm belief in a Creator God who
has a plan and a purpose and who stands in judgment of
those who turn away from that purpose is important for
all of us.

But, how does God accomplish his purpose? Do we have

to think of him as a divine genie who comes to the rescue when faithful believers are in trouble and when they say the right words or do the right things? Is he always stepping in to change the course of history so that the faithful will win? No, the Bible makes it clear that there were many times when faithful people had to suffer, when it appeared God had deserted them. Jesus said to his disciples, "In this world you will have tribulation." But, he also made it clear that they did not have to bear that tribulation by themselves. He went to the Cross to show how far God is willing to go in sharing suffering which is caused by evil men. Paul summed it up when he wrote, "In everything, God works for good with those who love him . . ." (Romans 8:28, RSV.)

But, how is that Divine presence felt? How does it really make a difference in my life or the life of my society? Dr. Albert Outler suggests that God's presence and power must be understood not as being like an engineer who prepares the perfect blueprints, nor like the skilled craftsman who builds the faultless machine; but rather, it is like the wise phychiatrist. He knows how to help his patient move to the place where he freely makes those decisions and does those things which enable him to be his best self. In other words, God actively maintains an order where creative, dynamic, human freedom is possible. Or, as Paul said to the Athenians, "He is not far from each one of us, for in him we live and move, in him we exist."

Dr. Outler expands this suggestion that God may be like the wise phychiatrist by pointing out that a good psychiatrist usually is quick to know where his patient's trouble lies. But he also knows that the best way to help is not always to step in and start telling him what to do and how he ought to feel. Rather, he has to create a climate of openness and trust, a sense of freedom, which will enable the patient to discover his own faults and weaknesses, to verbalize them, and to begin to take steps to correct them. For this to happen, Dr. Outler says, "there must not only be an atmosphere of intelligent love. There must also be a personal presence—a special sort of spiritual relation that is loving without being selfish, and understanding without being officious. This presence has also to be sensed by the patient for what it is, and *trusted* without dependence or resentment." [6] This kind of trust is what the Bible means by faith. This kind of loving presence is what it means by God's saving power or his providence.

We have said, then, that belief in the Creator God who was preached by Paul in Athens means at least two things. First, it means believing there is a transcendent power and purpose which is greater than anything we can completely comprehend. And it means that this purpose is the stand-ard, the Divine plumb line, by which all our man-made schemes are measured. And second, we have said this belief means trusting that this Divine purpose is at least as loving and as intelligent as a good psychiatrist who helps his patient move to the place where he freely makes those decisions and does those things which enable him to be his best self.

Now, if this is what we mean by belief in God, then worship makes sense. In worship, we come together to celebrate the privilege of life in such a universe. Nothing great or important can be taken for granted. Even the most obvious truths must be reaffirmed and rediscovered by each person, by each generation. So, in worship, we join in reaffirming these great facts about God. We strengthen, support, and encourage each other in remembering them. We sing about them. We confess our failure to live by them. We read about them from the Bible. We talk about them from the pulpit, in the hope that some new insight or some new truth may be inspired by such reading and discussion. We bow in prayer or we stand, to express our deep desire to be more faithful disciples. And in those moments when we truly reach beyond ourselves and com-mit ourselves to values and purposes which are beyond our complete understanding—in those moments we are more truly individuals than at any other time in our lives.

In other words, the true humanist is the person who sees something beyond the limits of human knowledge and understanding, something which he recognizes as that which makes being human possible. This is what happened to sociologist Peter Berger, and made him write, ". . . religion is not primarily an activity of intellectuals. . . . The fundamental religious impulse is not to theorize about transcendence but to worship it." [7] This also happened to science-philosopher Alfred Whitehead and which led him to write: "The power of God is the worship he inspires. That religion is strong which in its ritual and its modes of thought evokes an apprehension of the commanding vision."

It was this commanding vision of "one who does not live in shrines made by men" which Paul had and which he was proclaiming to the men of Athens. It is this same vision which we must keep before us today. "We recognize Him, says St. John of the Cross, because we carry in our hearts a rough sketch of the beloved countenance. Looking into these deeps, as into a quiet pool in the dark forest, we there find looking back at us the Face we implicitly long for and already know. It is set in another world, another light; yet it is here. As we realize this, our prayer widens until it embraces the extremes of awestruck adoration and confident love, and fuses them into one." [8]

SUGGESTIONS FOR GROUP STUDY

Commence this session by clarifying your understanding of the writer's ideas in this sermon. Refer to the suggestions in the box on page 8.

In pairs, discuss this question: How have you experienced God to be transcendent? In order to deal with this question, you and your partner will have to come to a clear understanding of "transcendence."

Now, join pairs together into groups of four, share your understandings of transcendence, and discuss this question: How would you answer a person who asked, "How can you believe in something you cannot fully understand?" Share insights from each team of four with the whole group. Can you as a whole group agree on some useful responses to the efforts to "have God all figured out" and "whittled down to human dimensions and human terms so we can all understand him?"

Discuss as a whole group: How does a misunderstanding of the transcendent nature of God contribute to a church "being more concerned with maintaining its rituals and forms than working for justice and righteousness in society?" Now reverse this question: In what specific ways have you seen an honest search for the kingdom of God lead directly to a ministry of social concern? How have you seen this take place in your own church?

The writer quotes Albert Outler as likening God not to an engineer or to a craftsman but to a psychiatrist. Ask each person in turn to complete this sentence: "I usually think of God as a_____because_____.
List on newsprint the different images of God identified by group members.

Conclude this session by sharing experiences of unusually deep or meaningful worship, then close by reading aloud together Psalm 8.

II

ALWAYS AT WORK

"My Father has never yet ceased his work, and I am working too." (John 5:17, NEB.)

A few years ago I was fortunate enough to see the Broadway production of Archibald McLeash's modern version of the Book of Job. In this play, where a successful American business man named "J.B." is the twentieth century counterpart of the biblical Job, God was portrayed as a man in black, standing on a balcony to the left of the stage. He never came down from that balcony. All he did was stand and look on, as J.B. faced one calamity after another. Well, long before the play was ended, I found myself exclaiming under my breath, "Why doesn't God do something? Why does he just stand there and let man suffer so?"

In recent years, as I have looked out on the terrific suffering, the injustices and inequalities, the seeming triumph of totalitarian regimes in our world, I have often found myself asking the same questions.

Jesus also lived in a critical time when men were asking similar questions. In desperation, he himself once cried, "My God, why?" But, when his true faith came through, he prayed, "Father, into thy hands I commend my spirit . . . Not my will but thine be done." On another occasion, Jesus put into one sentence the great and continuing affirmation of the entire Bible. He said, "My Father has never ceased his work, and I am working too."

There is a sense in which the entire Bible is simply an

expansion, a documentation of that affirmation. It begins
with the assertion that the world as we know it is God's
idea to begin with, that he identified himself with man's
struggle to understand and shape this world, that he bound
himself by a solemn covenant sealed with a rainbow never
to forsake humankind. It concludes with the picture of
the forces of righteousness and justice triumphing over
the forces of tyranny and oppression as a heavenly chorus
sings, "The Lord God omnipotent reigns! He shall reign
forever and ever!" In this song, the early Christians meant
what we mean when we sing, "He's got the whole world
in His hands."

The best exposition of this belief which I have seen is
a statement which was drawn up by an international
meeting of Christian leaders in Malay just before the out-
break of World War II. It is called the Tambaram Confession, after the name of the city where the meeting was
held. It says in part: "Above all and in all and through all
is the holy will, the creative purpose, of the Most High.
The world is His and He made it. The confusions of history
are in the grasp of His manifold wisdom. He overrules and
works through the purposes of men, bringing to nought
their stubborn and rebellious lust for power, but building
their fidelity into the structure of His reign upon earth."

There are three things which this confession is saying
and which Jesus also kept affirming throughout his ministry. They might be put this way: First, there is no situation, no matter how evil or hopeless it may seem, where
God is not present and where he is not at work. Second,
God is not leaving men to stew in their own juice. Third,
God is actually defeating evil. Let us look at each of these
affirmations.

First, we believe there is no situation, no matter how
evil or hopeless it may seem, where God is not present
and where He is not at work. The Psalmist wrote, "Surely
the wrath of man shall praise thee." (Psalm 76:10, RSV.)
There are numerous instances in the Bible which show
God using people who denied him, people who had never
heard about him, and even people who defied him, to get
his work done. Look, for instance at the forty-fifth chap-

ter of Isaiah. God is shown speaking to Cyrus, the pagan king of the Persians. He certainly was not a Christian, not even a Jew. For a modern paralel, you might have to substitute a name like Mao Tse-tung or Ho Chi Minh. Isaiah wrote: "Thus says the Lord to his anointed, to Cyrus (the word "anointed" is the same word which we translate "ordained") I am the Lord, and there is no other, beside me there is no God; *I gird you, though you do not know me,* that men may know, from the rising of the sun and from the west, there is none beside me."

All of this simply means that while God may not have anything to do with the trouble we get ourselves into, He still is able to use even the worst of situations to accomplish His purposes. The supreme example of this fact is the crucifixion of Jesus. From every human standpoint, Jesus' death on the Cross was the worst situation which could be imagined; and yet, God was able to change the Cross from a sign of shame and defeat to a symbol of honor and victory.

You will remember that Pollyanna was one who could always see something good even in the worst situation. God can not only see something good; He is also able to bring something good out of any situation. As Paul wrote, "In everything God works for good . . . (Romans 8:28, RSV.) He is not, as some would have us believe, sitting back somewhere waiting to swoop down and set up a new heaven and a new earth overnight. He is not waiting for the end of time. He is present in every moment of time. And His presence is the creating, renewing, sustaining power which keeps us from completely wrecking our lives and our world. For the Bible, the question is never IF God is, it is seldom WHO God is; it is always WHERE God is. And the answer is always; God is where things are happening. He is where the action is!

At first sight, it is difficult to see God at work in the present situation; and yet, I believe there are some very real indications that He is very much at work right now. It may even be that He will be able to use Communism to accomplish His purposes, just as He used Cyrus and the Persians to accomplish His purposes 2,500 years ago.

Communism's double-talk about equality and economic freedom for the masses is an absurd caricature of the real equality and freedom which can be found through Christ; and yet, the very fact that so many millions of the Third World people are accepting this double-talk and are turning to some form of Communism in desperation may be God's way of making Christians put up or shut up. It may be His way of making us set our house in order so that we can prove our real concern for these ideals of equality, freedom, justice which we have followed afar off. In other words, God may be using Communism to spur us into making our economic and political system more Christian.

And then, the amazing advances of modern science and technology have brought the nations of the world so close together that we have to pay some attention to the welfare of others if we ourselves are to prosper and be happy. Whether we like it or not, science has moved all of us into a global village. Now, I don't think anyone would suggest that the scientists who perfected the Atomic and Hydrogen bombs or the inter-continental ballistic missiles had any altruistic or godly motive in mind. In fact, they and many who directed them had in mind the wholesale destruction of thousands of God's children. And yet, I firmly believe that the very interdependence of men and nations which has been forced upon us by these terrible weapons may be God's way of revealing His will and His way in the affairs of men. Dr. Arthur Compton, one of the scientists who had much to do with the creation of the Atomic bomb, said, "The development of the atomic bomb is merely the most recent important step of that steady progression of science that is compelling man to become human. Now he must pay careful attention to co-operation, education, and the welfare of society if he is to thrive under the conditions that science imposes." It is so clear that God has had a great deal to do with this trend toward interdependence which science has made imperative. It is clear there is no situation which God cannot and does not turn to his own advantage. "The confusions of history are in the grasp of his manifold wisdom!"

Thus, it is clear, in the second place, that God is not

leaving men to stew in their own juice. He is not a distant
and divine judge who has laid down certain laws; and
who now stands off on a balcony somewhere watching
men suffer as they break those laws. This was what the
great philosopher Immanuel Kant had in mind when he
wrote, "Thinking of God simply as an architect of the
world is not enough to form the basis of religion." No, of
course it is not enough. Man desperately craves and needs
assurance that he is not alone in his struggle against evil.
The New Testament teaches that God sent Jesus into the
world to give that assurance. It teaches that even as the
Son of God became a man, even as he faced the temptations, the trials and the sufferings of a man, the cruel
death and torture of the Cross, so God himself enters into
these human experiences. Paul wrote to that tiny band
of Christians facing persecution in the pagan city of Rome,
"We know that in everything God works for good with
those who love him. . . . If God is for us, who is against
us? . . . Who shall separate us from the love of Christ?
Shall tribulation, or distress, or persecution, or famine, or
nakedness, or peril, or sword? . . . No, in all these things
we are more than conquerors through him who loved us."
So it was that these first century Christians, as they
prayed the prayer Jesus had taught his apostles, began
adding the words, "for Thine is the kingdom, the power,
and the glory forever!"

But, it is still difficult always to realize that God is by
our side, is actually seeking to guide and strengthen us as
we travel life's rough roads. The main reason for this is
the fact that most men do not recognize God when he
does take a hand in their life. Augustine wrote, "I sought
thee at a distance, and did not know thou wast near. I
sought thee abroad, and behold thou wast within me." We
need to remember that one of the main instruments which
God uses to reveal himself is the voice of conscience. This
is the best way he has of saving men from sham and
cowardice, meanness and cruelty; and yet, there are many
of us who have stifled the voice of conscience so often
and so ruthlessly that we have what Shakespeare called
"a conscience as wide as hell." In that case, God has to

use other ways of directing and helping us. Many of the
Old Testament prophets seemed to be teaching that God
deliberately sent suffering and disaster upon such people
as a means of forcing them to turn to him. The God of the
New Testament is not that kind of deity; but he is a God
whose father heart is so broken by the suffering which
men bring upon themselves through their sins that he is
always ready to step in and share their suffering with
them. God does not deliberately cause men to suffer; but
he does speak to them through their suffering.

Every one of us have had the experience of feeling that
we are closer to God at some time of great sorrow or disappointment than at any other time in our lives. This is
not just a feeling. It is a fact. God actually does use these
sorrows and disappointments as doorways into men's
lives. Our barriers and defenses are down then more than
at any other time. We are more like little children then
than at any other time; and so, God has a much better
chance of being accepted as our Father. Arnold Toynbee,
the great historian, says that he sees little chance for
progress in the future except by way of the learning that
comes through the suffering which brings persons in
closer communion with God and makes them become less
unlike him. At a time when he was facing all kinds of
personal difficulties, when he was being maligned and
misinterpreted by whites and blacks alike, Dr. Martin
Luther King Jr. wrote, "God has been profoundly real to
me in recent years. In the midst of outer dangers I have
felt an inner calm. In the midst of lonely days and dreary
nights I have heard an inner voice saying, 'Lo, I will be
with you.' . . . I am convinced that the universe is under
the control of a loving purpose, and that in the struggle
for righteousness man has cosmic companionship. Behind
the harsh appearances of the world there is a benign
power." [9]

Yes, God does speak to men through their suffering. He
is speaking to them and seeking to guide them through
their conscience. But, he is also speaking to men through
the living words of the Bible. If you ever reach the point
where you doubt God's presence and his interest in you,

go back to this great book, especially the Psalms and the New Testament. It is hard to explain just how God speaks through these ancient words; and yet, I'm sure almost everyone has had the experience of feeling that a particular verse of a certain passage was speaking right to a personal need. Perhaps it was one Sunday when a preacher was reading the scripture lesson. It may have been sometime when a Choir was singing some great scripture passage which had been set to music—remember John Wesley's feeling about the singing of Psalm 130 in St. Paul's on the day of his Aldersgate experience? Or, perhaps this feeling came some morning when you read the verse printed at the top of the page in THE UPPER ROOM; but, whenever it was, there was a time when the words from this Book struck fire in your heart even as sparks fly when steel is struck against flint. And so, men who read this Book regularly are the ones who most often have the living flame of God's love in their hearts. The very existence of such a book is ample proof of the fact that God is not leaving men to stew in their own juice, but is doing everything he possibly can to save men from their sins and to bring them into the full and abundant life which can be seen in the teachings of this book and in the life of Christ.

One final thing must be said about God. It is this: God is going to win. He is defeating evil. As the Tambaran confession says, "He overrules and works through the purposes of men, bringing to nought their stubborn and rebellious lust for power, but building their fidelity into the structure of his reign upon earth." There are times we are tempted to doubt this, and to feel that God is being defeated. Such was the feeling throughout Europe when the armies of Napoleon were sweeping all opposition before them. But, there came a time when even Napoleon was defeated. God's part in that defeat was stated with great incite by Victor Hugo. He wrote, "Was it possible for Napoleon to win the battle? No. Why? Not on account of Wellington, and not on account of Blucher, but on account of God. Bonaparte a victor at Waterloo did not harmonize with a law of the universe which was preparing an order in which Napoleon had no place. . . . It was in Infinitude that Napoleon had been denounced and his fall decreed. "Waterloo was not merely a battle; it was a trend of the universe."

Of course, this trend toward the ultimate triumph of truth and right does not mean that God can always prevent evil men from acquiring great power. As long as men have freedom to choose the way they are going, God cannot prevent the misuse of that freedom. If we lie and call it diplomacy, if we enslave and call it liberation, if we exploit and call it equality, if we bomb and incinerate helpless thousands of women and children and call it a defense of freedom—if we choose to act in these ways, God cannot prevent us, or at least he does not, since he is unwilling to take back the freedom he has bestowed and turn us into mechanical robots. But God can and does maintain the moral order of the universe. The very disasters which have come upon our fathers and upon us— economic depression, mass unemployment, two world wars, wars in the Middle East and in the Far East, rioting in our cities, pollution of our planet—all of these simply emphasize the fact that there is a just God in control of things. If we had been able to continue our short-sighted and selfish ways without facing such disasters, then there would be real reason to doubt the existence and the power of a God of justice and love. Sooner or later, in one way or another, men and nations have to live through the consequences of their sins. The psalmist wrote:

> God says, "Through all the long delay
> I am still ruling in my justice;
> When men in panic melt away,
> I still uphold the order of the world."
>
> Psalm 75 (Moffat)

This simply means we can have peace if we do the will of God, and only if we do his will. This is the great lesson which history teaches. It is the great lesson which the Bible teaches. Above all, it is the great lesson which is taught by the life, the death, and the resurrection of Jesus Christ.

I wonder how long it will take men to learn this lesson? There are some who have learned it well. They are the ones who work steadily on when others succumb to mental lassitude and despair. They are the ones who undertake constructive projects when the world is going to pieces all about them. They are the ones who see that insoluble problems are often disguised opportunities. In a word, these are the ones who hold the world together. They are the ones I would ask you to join, not by gritting your teeth and clinching your fists; but by relaxing your nerves, bowing your heads and saying, "Oh, Lord, I believe; help my unbelief. I know you are still at work. Let me be at work with you."

SUGGESTIONS FOR GROUP STUDY

Begin this session by focusing on the writer's statements and ideas. Be sure you understand these by following one or more of the suggestions in the box on page 8.

In order to learn from this sermon, apply it to practical situations in the lives of the members of the group. Try this: Divide your group into three teams. Direct the members of each team to share personal experiences with the other members of the team, one team discussing experiences in which God seemed not to be present, the second team sharing experiences in which persons felt God had left "men to stew in their own juice," and the third team describing personal experiences of times when God seemed not to be defeating evil. As team members share experiences, let each team member answer questions such as these about his or her shared experience: Why did this experience seem especially significant to you? What did you do in this situation to try to rediscover God and his will within this situation? How, if at all, did your understanding of God and his nature change as a result of this situation? What most helped you through this situation?

Let each team share especially significant experiences with the whole group.

Now, try applying some of the sermon's insights to

some real life situations. Role play these situations, allowing time following each role play for discussion:

• A teenager comes to you and says, "There isn't any God. If there were, he wouldn't have let my father die in the car accident!"

• A Sunday school class member says to three of you, "I don't know why we have to worry about war and poverty and pollution. God is taking care of all these, isn't he?"

• A middle-aged mother talks with two of her friends: "Well, my son went and got himself in trouble with the police. I certainly can't forgive him, and I'm sure God doesn't either. He got himself into this mess; he can just get himself out of it!"

• A member of a minority group talks with two men at work: "I've always been poor and sick, and I always will be. I guess it's what God has planned for me."

Remember: You are seeking helpful answers for the persons in these situations; if the persons in the situations do not feel comforted by your answers, they should say so.

Conclude this session by sharing experiences of unexpected blessing that you have attributed to God's love. Then read aloud together Romans 8:38-39 and offer sentence prayers for understanding of God's will for your life.

III

MAN IS INTENDED TO LIVE AS JESUS LIVED

"Behold the man." (John 19:5.) "I find in him, no fault at all." (John 19:6, KJV.)

Americans have long prided themselves on their virile manliness. To many this has meant a sense of independence, a sturdy conviction of personal worth which refuses to be pushed around by anyone. But, for many others, it has meant primarily a stubborn persistence which refuses to back down on anything or ever to admit that one has been wrong.

Back during those tense days when President Nixon expanded the Vietnam war by sending troops into Cambodia, a White House aide was attempting to explain this action to a group of reporters. He said, "The President had to show the world that America hasn't lost its manhood."

What do you think he meant by that? How *do* we affirm our manhood as a nation, as citizens? What does it mean to be a man?

For centuries, philosophers have tried to define the meaning of manhood; and in more recent years, they have been joined by psychologists and psychiatrists. Plato said the good man has four cardinal virtues: fortitude, equity, prudence, and temperance. Psychiatrists talk about manhood as being well-adjusted.

But, the message of the Bible is that God has given us something much better than philosophical or psychological definitions. It says that in Jesus of Nazareth He has given us a model of true manhood. John quotes Pontius Pilate as pointing to Jesus and saying, "Behold the man . . . I find in him, no fault at all." And in another place John quotes the burly temple police who were sent out to arrest Jesus, coming back empty-handed, saying "No man ever spoke like this man." They had met their match—one who by the sheer strength of his character triumphed over their military and physical strength. Paul, in his letters, referred to Jesus as the "second Adam." In other words, the man Jesus was as perfect as the first man created by God. Here is God's original blueprint for man—what God had in mind when he first created man.

Several years ago, when the Rockefeller Foundation set out to restore the original buildings of old Williamsburg, the colonial capital of Virginia, they were eager to make them as exact as possible. One of the first and most important was to be the original building of William and Mary College. Part of the building was still in use, but it had been altered quite a bit. After extensive research, the historians finally found in an old English library a copper plate picture which showed the original plan of that building as it had been designed by Sir Christopher Wren in 1690. This was just what they needed; and today, you can see that building restored precisely as it was designed. In the same way, I am suggesting that those who want to know what God had in mind when he created man have only to look at man as he can be seen in Jesus of Nazareth. Clearly, man is intended to live as Jesus lived.

It is particularly important that we take such a look today because many are feeling as Dr. Martin Niemoller felt after he was released from several years confinement in a Nazi concentration camp. Someone asked him if he had lost faith in God. He replied, "No, but I have lost faith in man." Undoubtedly the beastliness to which men sank during the days of World War II and to which they have continued to sink in the Korean and the Vietnam wars has made many people lose faith in man. Many would say of all men what the psychiatrist said to one of his patients. "Madame," he said, "You don't have an inferiority complex. You *are* inferior." In Jesus' day, there was a common saying, "Can any good come out of Nazareth?" In our day, many are saying, in effect, "Can any good come out of man?" In the name of freedom, they describe man as the creature of heredity and environment. Or they say his actions are determined by his glands, or by his subconscious. Still others say it is economic necessity which is the determining factor in the lives of men. So, in effect, they say, "Why worry. You are the creature of forces you cannot control. Don't sweat it! Live it up! Let nature take its course." Of course, the truth is that there is no freedom here at all. Man is turned into an automated machine or an instinct-driven animal.

At the other extreme, there are those who are trying to substitute for man, the concept of "Superman." In various forms, this has been the basic belief of Marx, Lenin, Mussolini, Hitler, Mao Tse-tung, and all other totalitarian leaders. In one form or another they have propounded the belief that the possibilities of human achievement are unlimited. But this has also been the prime doctrine of materialistic capitalism. So, there is a very real sense in which the religion of "Superman" may have become the chief competitor of Christianity.

What are we to do? Are these extremes our only choice? The choice seems to be between a pessimistic nihilism or neo-orthodoxy which sees no good in man whatever or the naive notion of "Superman" which assumes there is no limit to what man can do, in his own power.

That is the reason the Christian message about the birth and the life of Jesus Christ is so very important today. But, its real meaning can be comprehended only if we will read our New Testaments as if we were reading them for the first time. I think that is what Soren Kierkegaard was doing when he wrote, "When I read the New Testament, I get the impression that in God's opinion every man is a giant. . . . How ironical that every man is designed to be an Atlas, capable of bearing the weight of the world—and then to see what men we are; . . ." [10] This is the real paradox of the Christian gospel, isn't it? In Jesus Christ, God gives us a picture of man as he was meant to be—the original blueprint; but, then, through the cruelty of the crucifixion, He also gives us a picture of man at his lowest and his worst. And, as we see ourselves among the crucifiers, or as we compare ourselves to the perfection described in the Sermon on the Mount, we feel that there is no hope for us. Pascal wrote, "Christianity is strange. It bids man recognize that he is vile, even abominable; and then bids him desire to be like God." What is the way out of this dilemma? Is there really any good news (gospel) here for modern man?

Of course, I believe there is or I wouldn't have been preaching the gospel from a pulpit for more than thirty years. It is the good news which begins with the clear declaration that such a man as Jesus of Nazareth actually lived on this earth, and that we have sufficient reliable information about him to understand what he did and what he was. Many efforts have been made to prove that such a person never really existed; but all such efforts have been discredited and every advance in the historical criticism of the Gospels has tended to confirm the basic and important facts they proclaim. It is quite true we do not have in any sense of the word what modern historians would consider to be an authentic biography of Jesus. We have nothing that he wrote. The brief pictures from his life are accounts written by men who may never have seen him in the flesh—men whose great purpose was to proclaim a faith and not to outline a life. For this reason, scholars like Dibelius and Bultmann have made it clear that the accounts of Jesus' life have been highly colored by the faith of those who wrote. But, this does not mean that all the facts are suspect—that none of them can be trusted. Dr. Leander Keck wrote recently in his book, *A Future For The Historical Jesus,* "While we cannot know Jesus as completely as we once may have thought, we can know important things solidly." [11] Few books have been studied as critically and as minutely as have the books of the New Testament. Every possible effort has been made to discredit them and to prove them false; but in spite of these efforts, certain basic facts can be authenticated as much as the fact that Alexander the Great led his army in conquering the world or that Julius Caesar was a great Roman Emperor. These things we know as surely as it is possible for men to know: Jesus was born in Palestine during the reign of Herod the Great. He was brought up in Nazareth. He lived the normal life of a Jew of his period and locale. He was baptized by John, a proclaimer of the early coming of God's judgment. He spent a year or more in teaching groups of his fellow countrymen in various parts of Palestine, mostly in Galilee, and in more intimate association with some chosen friends and disciples. He incurred the hostility of some of his compatriots and the suspicion of the Roman authorities. He was put to death in Jerusalem by those same authorities during the procuratorship of Pilate.[12]

But, we know more. We not only know that the man, Jesus of Nazareth, existed. We also know a good deal about what kind of man he was. And this is most important to our faith. Remember that the earliest traditions about Jesus were written down within fifty years after his birth—that the greater part of the New Testament was written within fifty years after his death. Even more important, there are in the New Testament at least six different interpretations of Jesus. They differ markedly in detail and in point of view; but the overwhelming impression left as you read them is that all these writers were trying to depict the same person, and that that person was unlike anyone else who has ever lived in the world.[13]

For those who continue to insist that the character, Jesus, was invented or fabricated, Bishop Stephen Neill points out that the character we meet in the New Testament is not at all the kind of person we would expect those first century writers to have invented. "He did not fulfill any of the messianic expectations that were current among the Jews of his day. He is not in the least like any of the savior-gods of the contemporary Mediterranean mythology. As Paul himself so frankly tells us, what the Christians preached was absurdity to the intelligent Greeks, and a scandal to tradition-minded Jews." And so,

if these New Testament authors were going to invent a
God-man, this is not what they would have come up with.
"If they set things down as they did . . . it is obvious they
did so only because they could not escape from a reality
they had not created and that imposed itself upon them." [14]

Yes, this man did live; and the fact that he lived makes
life for you and me meaningful and desirable. Often you
hear the expression, "It's only human." What do we mean
by this? Usually this is used as an excuse for something
we know is less than ideal. For instance, a minister is on
the eighteenth hole on the golf course. He is leading with
a good score. He steps up to the tee, swings and slices his
ball into the rough. Impulsively, he explodes with some
choice theological words which are clearly out of context.
So, his companions laughingly say to one another, "After
all, he is only human." Or, a business man cuts a few
corners in order to make a better profit; and his fellow
business men excuse him and themselves by saying,
"After all, he is only human." Or again, a high school football player who has been goaded beyond endurance by an
opposing linesman finally starts slugging him, when the
referee isn't looking. Some of the spectators see it, but they
excuse him by saying, "After all, he is only human." But,
we need to re-examine this accepted interpretation of
what it means to be human. What is a genuinely human
existence?

Strangely enough, Dr. Karl Barth, the man who many
feel has done much to degrade our theological concept of
man is the one who has also given a definition of human
existence I want you to think about. He wrote, "Man is
the creature made visible in the mirror of Jesus Christ." [15]
In other words, if you want to know what it means to be
human, look at Jesus Christ. Here God has given us a
living picture of man that can never be erased or forgot-
ten, no matter how cruel or beastly other men may be. As
G. K. Chesterton put it, "We were to hear no more the
wail of Ecclesiastes that humanity had no pre-eminence
over the brute, or the awful cry of Homer that man was
only the saddest of all the beasts of the field. Man was a
statue of God walking about the garden." [16] The Gospel

of John says, "The expression of God became a human
being and lived among us. We saw His splendor, full of
grace and truth." (John 1:14, Philips.) So, I ask that we
look at ourselves in the mirror which God has given us in
Jesus Christ. What kind of man was he?

He was first of all a man of power. "The Jesus who
strides through the Gospels is a man of immense and terri-
fying power. He is the master of every situation. He is a
long way from the gentle Jesus, meek and mild we see in
stained-glass windows and sing about in sentimental
hymns. There were times when even his closest friends
were awed by his moral and intellectual power. He seemed
to be the master of every situation, from stilling the storm
on the Sea of Galilee to walking straight through the mob
in Nazareth. He spoke with such authority and power that
the burly temple police were afraid to lay a hand on him;
and the calloused Roman Centurion who had seen many
men die on a cross exclaimed, "Surely, this man was the
Son of God." But, this sense of power came not so much
from any weird, supernatural, magic that men saw in him.
Rather, they seemed to sense the moral authority of the
man. His strength was clear because the rightness and the
justice of his words and his life were clear. Tennyson
wrote of Sid Galahad that his "strength was as the strength
of ten because his heart was pure." This, of course, was
the secret of Jesus' power. This is what made him the
strongest of men.

But, along with this power and strength, there was in
this man an unshakable goodwill toward all men. Evidently there was nothing which could make him wish evil
for other men. Now, it's true his compassionate concern
for the underprivileged sometimes made him righteously
indignant toward those who cheated them or laid unnec-
essary burdens on them—as when he drove the money-
changers out of the temple or when he denounced the
self-righteous Scribes who tithed even the herb in their
gardens but cheated poor widows out of their homes. But,
still he sought the best even for such persons as these.
Remember the time he stood on the Mount of Olives looking out over the city of Jerusalem, knowing all about the

wickedness and evil intentions of its leaders. Still, he wept over the city, exclaiming, "O Jerusalem, Jerusalem! You kill the prophets and stone the messengers God has sent you! How many times I have wanted to put my arms around all you people, just as a hen gathers her chicks under her wings, but you would not let me!" (Matthew 33:37, TEV.) The same enduring goodwill was expressed in his prayer from the Cross: "Father, forgive them for they know not what they do." This indestructible goodwill was described by John's gospel, "Having loved his own, he loved them to the end." (John 13:7, RSV.) It was summed up by Paul when he wrote, "Love bears all things, believes all things, hopes all things, endures all things." (I Corinthians 13:7, RSV.) In Somerset Maugham's novel *The Razor's Edge* there is a young man who is described as one who loved with a cool passion. Perhaps it's overly romantic to think that a man can be both passionate and cool at the same time; and yet, this comes close to describing this enduring goodwill of Jesus. He cared passionately for the rights of the little guy, for the human instead of the abstract, for the truth instead of the popular; but he never allowed his passion to make him "lose his cool."

But along with Jesus' goodwill and his power, there was an unlimited humility and willingness to serve. So often, men of power are led into arrogance and disregard of the rights of others. As Lord Acton said, "Power corrupts." But, this was not true in Jesus. Even his disciples found it difficult to understand his unwillingness to let them put him up in the place of honor and respect which they felt a man of such power and strength should have. In those days, there were many teachers or rabbis who had a retinue of disciples following them around, memorizing their words, seeking to learn from them, acting as servants to them. But, Jesus refused to let his disciples follow this accepted pattern. Instead of their washing his feet, he insisted on washing their feet. He contrasted the way men of great political power ordered men around with their relation to him and to each other. He said, "This is not the way it is with you; rather, the greatest one among you must be like the youngest, and the leader must be like the

servant . . . I am among you as one who serves." (Luke
22:26-27, TEV.) Jesus has been called "the man for others."

He was a leader of men—one who tolerated no half-
hearted followers. He made all-out demands on his disciples. Yet, he never had the appearance of self-seeking or
self-assertion. Men somehow sensed that his demand for
total obedience rested upon his own total obedience to
One higher than himself.

He was a judge of men and yet there was almost a
womanly gentleness about his character. His denunciation
of the hypocrites was unequaled in its severity; but,
along with this, there was this unlimited concern for sinners. The man who condemns the wickedness of Jerusalem,
also weeps over it. His judgments are severe but you
know they are so only because the truth he serves cannot
be denied or ignored.

Still, he was not an austere man. He was most friendly
and accessible. It is clear that he really enjoyed the society
of ordinary people. He attended their wedding feasts,
their banquets, their synagogue services. He was no remote ascetic like John the Baptist. And yet, along with
this out-going friendliness, there was also an urgent need
to be alone, for he was a man of prayer. Even when multi-
tudes were pressing upon him, he withdrew to a mountain
for prayer. In fact, this was such an essential part of his
life that when the disciples came to him, they did not say,
"Teach us to be courageous, or teach us to be humble, or
teach us to be friendly." They said, "Teach us to pray."

This was the man whose life actually split history into
two sections—before and after. We could go on and on
listing his unique characteristics; but this is enough to
illustrate the truth we are affirming: each quality of human life is present here in the highest degree possible,
but without destroying contrasting or contrary qualities.
It would seem that God himself was speaking through
Pilate when he said, "Behold the man"; or "Behold man—
man as I intend him to be."

But having said this, I must caution that there is some
danger in drawing this or any other idealized portrait of
what a man ought to be. Evidently it is God's plan that

each person should be unique and different from every other person. So there is danger in trying to set up a mold which shapes all persons alike, even if that mold is named "Jesus." There is danger in judging men by preconceived labels or categories. Just when you seem to have a person defined, categorized, identified once and for all, then he does something that seems unexplainable. A husband who has been married to the same woman for forty years and who thinks he knows her pretty well, often finds himself exclaiming, "What in the world made her do that?" Even psychiatrists are beginning to realize that they cannot categorize and label people. Dr. Karl Menninger has led the way in insisting that psychiatrists must treat each person as a person rather than as a schizophrenic or neurotic, or homosexual or whatever other label might be applied. So too, we must be careful not to start labeling people and deciding whether they can be squeezed into a certain "Jesus-Mold." We may say that the Christian man is meek, compassionate, courageous, persistent, forgiving; but who is to judge when meekness becomes cowardice, courage becomes obstinacy and egotism?

Still, if it is true that a man lived as Jesus lived, there is new hope for each one of us. It means, as Paul wrote, that "the whole creation is on tiptote to see the wonderful sight of the sons of God coming into their own." (Romans 8:19, Phillips.) Much of the emptiness of modern life is due to the fact that there is no clear vision of what man is meant to be. "We are being stifled by an outlook which makes us cogs in a machine." [17] But, through the birth, the life, the teachings of Jesus Christ, God is calling us back to the original blueprint. He is saying, "This is what I want you to be. This is what I will help you to become. Only believe in him. Only trust in me."

At one time, Sweden's most famous violinist was a man named Ole Bull. He had a friend named Ericsson who was a skilled craftsman but who insisted that he had no ear for music. So he would never attend Bull's concerts. But one day Ole's violin was badly damaged in an accident. He brought it to his friend to be repaired. Ericsson soon had it almost better than new. Ole put it under his chin to test it; and as he played, workmen from all over the shop gathered to hear the lovely strains of music. At first, Ericsson appeared indifferent; but as his friend continued, his look of indifference changed to one of enchantment. And, finally, he cried out, "Ole, Ole, I've got an ear for music after all!"

It is in some such way as this that God pushes through the indifference and pretended hardness of man. In the man, Christ Jesus, he makes us see ourselves as we really are. He makes us revise our low estimate of ourselves. He makes us see that we have an ear for music after all— the music which he has written, the music whose score we can read in that man of Nazareth. And so, we find ourselves praying, "Have thine own way, Lord. Have thine own way. Thou art the potter, I am the clay. Mold me and make me after thy will, while I am waiting, yielded and still."

SUGGESTIONS FOR GROUP STUDY

Begin this session by dealing with the content of this sermon. The material in the box on page 8 offers some suggestions for doing this.

Supply paper and pencils for group members, then ask each person to write what he or she considers to be the five most important characteristics a person might have. In other words, what five characteristics would a person have if he or she were to be the very best possible person he or she could be? Then ask each person to write a brief paragraph indicating how he or she came to believe that each of the five characteristics is central in human personality. For example, one person might list: "Honesty— my father taught me since I was a child to be absolutely honest in everything."

Now share your lists of characteristics and the sources of your lists. Write the various characteristics on the chalkboard or newsprint. Did any characteristic appear on all lists? Which characteristics appeared on only one or two lists? Why do you think this is so?

Now examine the total list of characteristics: How many

and which of these characteristics do you see reflected in the life of Jesus Christ? Can you cite examples from the gospels of all these characteristics in the life of Jesus? Which of the group's list of characteristics is *not* a characteristic of the life of Jesus? Should a person seek to cultivate a characteristic that he or she does not find in the life of Jesus? Explain your answer as fully as possible, citing examples and illustrations where appropriate.

Divide your group into three teams and divide your list of characteristics equally among the three teams. [If not already included in the list of characteristics, assign one team the characteristic "power and strength," a second team "goodwill toward all persons," and the third team "humility and willingness to serve." These, of course, are three characteristics of Jesus taken from this sermon.] Each team is to 1) discuss the meaning of each of its assigned characteristics in terms of everyday life: How can one act with Christlike power and strength in everyday life; and 2) discuss specific ways in which persons today can grow in each of the characteristics assigned: What, specifically, can I do to grow in humility, to increase my willingness to serve?

Allow time for each of the three teams to make a full report to the whole group and for the group to respond to each report.

Conclude this session by singing together "Have Thine Own Way, Lord," number 154 in *The Book Hymns (The Methodist Hymnal)*, then individually offer sentence prayers of commitment and dedication.

IV

THE STRANGER OF GALILEE

"He had no form or comeliness that we should look at him, and no beauty that we should desire him." (Isaiah 53:2.)
"Do not think that I have come to bring peace on earth; I have not come to bring peace, but a sword." (Matthew 10:34.)
"I have come into the world to bear witness to the truth." (John 18:37.)

What is the first picture that comes to your mind when someone speaks of Jesus Christ? If you were an artist what kind of portrait would you paint? Do you think of him primarily in terms of the well-loved hymn, "What a friend we have in Jesus?" Is your main concept of Jesus illustrated by the words of another hymn: "He walks with me, he talks with me, he tells me I am his own?" Do you think of Jesus as someone who is always pleasant to be around, someone who helps you do what you want done, someone who never crosses you?

If so, what has the Church meant when it has described him with the words of the prophet: "He had no form or comeliness that we should look at him, and no beauty that we should desire him. He was despised and rejected by men"? What did Jesus mean when he said, "Do not think that I have come to bring peace on earth; I have not come to bring peace, but a sword"? What did he mean when he said, "I have come into the world to bear witness to the truth"? Usually we have thought of Jesus as coming into the world to save men from anxiety and fear, to bring peace of mind, comfort.

There is a very real sense in which he did. It is not a hollow promise when he said, "Come unto me all ye who labor and are heavy laden and I will give you rest." During his lifetime, there were many who through him found that their burdens were lifted. There was the blind Bartimaeus. There was the lame man by the pool of Siloam. There was the adulteress he saved from stoning. There was the Samaritan woman by the well whom he saved from herself. There was Mary Magdalen whose life was so changed she wiped his feet with her hair. These and scores more were given real comfort and new peace of mind.

But there were just as many who found him to be a terribly troubling, disturbing, upsetting person for them. Even his parents found him to be a strange boy to understand. They couldn't understand why a twelve-year-old boy would be so concerned to question the Scribes in the Temple. His neighbors in Nazareth were at first startled by his speaking ability in the Synagogue. They exclaimed, "Isn't this the son of the Carpenter?" Later, they were shocked and angered by his words, so that they tried to kill him. His mother and his brothers tried to call him away from his ministry. One Gospel says they thought he was out-of-his mind. Peter was drawn to him almost in spite of himself; but it was not always a comforting experience for him. His first response was, "Depart from me, for I am a sinful man." And I'm sure Peter did not feel very comfortable when Jesus rebuked him at Caesarea Phillippi, "Get behind me, Satan. You are not on the side of God." Other disciples had similar experiences. The rich young ruler turned away from him "sorrowfully." He had not found the comfort and acceptance he expected. The Church leaders of his day, the Scribes and Pharisees, were completely frustrated and angered by his rejection of their legalisms. Even the common people who, at first, flocked to hear him grew puzzled, and finally turned away either in indifference or in anger when he refused to accept the role of the miraculous military messiah they anticipated. Carl Quimby stated it well when he wrote, "Jesus was not only his day's most stirring character, but its most hated hero." [18] He was the "Stranger of Galilee." While he was the most human of men, there was also an unfathomable mystery about him which often left men awed, frightened, and angered.

What was there about this man who lived such a genuinely human existence that made him such a mysterious stranger? Well, for one thing, the *ideas* he taught seemed strange and unacceptable to many. In a day of militant political nationalism, he talked about a Kingdom based upon brotherhood and good will. In an age which thought of material prosperity as proof of God's blessing, he talked about such rewards as carrying a cross. In a Roman world built upon force, he urged self-effacing gentleness that turned the other cheek. In a society which often measured greatness by how many slaves or servants a man could command, he said the greatest man is the one who is servant of all. He said the meek would inherit the earth.

What was even more disturbing and strange, his life was a complete demonstration of his ideas. What he said he did. His words and his deeds were one. When throngs of people wanted to crown him as King, he slipped away from them. He renounced all insignia of power, lived with stark simplicity and utter self-effacement. He treated all men as his brothers, refusing even to separate himself from those who were considered foul sinners. He would not even follow the common practice of letting his pupils wait upon him. Instead, he took a towel, a basin of water, and washed their feet.

It is not surprising that men felt baffled in his presence. "At Capernaum the people wondered, at Bethany they argued, on the open sea they whispered, 'What manner of man is this?' There was something about Him that made men stop and stare. Men found Him hard to label, harder still to classify, to explain, to ignore. He just did not 'belong.' " [19]

But today, we sing, "What a friend we have in Jesus!" We croon, "He walks with me, he talks with me, he tells me I am his own." Is it possible that this may be our way

of refusing to face up to his real demands on our lives?
The more like us we picture him as being, the less like
him we will have to be. In one of W. H. Auden's poems
he has this line:

"O God, put aside justice and truth . . .
  You know we cannot understand or accept them . . .
  Be weak like us, and we'll understand you."

But, no matter how hard we try, God will not let us treat
Him that way. In Jesus Christ there is a truth, a justice, a
rightness that cannot and will not be twisted or turned or
watered down to fit our human categories. This was true
in his day. It is still true today.

The other day, I ran across a speech which was given
by a Church editor to a Young Republican Club in Asheville, North Carolina. One of the things he said was,
"Coexistence of Christianity with communism is impossible without tension." I'm sure they must have applauded
this statement. It is certainly true; but there is a further
truth which I did not find in his speech. He did not go on
to say, "Christianity cannot coexist with the Asheville
Young Republican Club without tension?" He did not
point out that there is bound to be tension between
Christianity and any human institution, political party, or
form of government. Even as Christ was so great and so
good that he was in tension with the social, the political,
the religious institutions of his day; so, there is bound to
be tension today. By its very nature Christianity cannot
coexist without tension with the Rotary Club, the Demo-
cratic Party, the American Medical Association, the C.I.O.,
the P.T.A., the Y.M.C.A., the N.A.A.C.P., The United Methodist Church or with any denomination or church. Christianity never stamps "approved" on what is; because of
Christ, there is always something better to become, something greater to do.

One of the greatest dangers which faces true religion
is not that of open warfare with obvious enemies. The
greater danger is that it will slowly but surely accommo-
date and adjust to the subtle pressures of society so that
in time the Christian Church becomes a tame, "kept" insti-

tution. History is replete with examples of just this very thing. Constantine used the Church to bless his slaughter and conquest of tribesmen who opposed the expansion of the Roman Empire. In the Middle Ages, Kings connived with Popes to play the game of power politics on the continent of Europe; and, in the name of Christ, to slaughter the Moslems in the Holy Land. In the fifteenth and sixteenth centuries, Cortez, Coronado and others destroyed and plundered the Indians of North and South America— all in the name of Christ and for the glory of the Church. In the nineteenth century, here in the United States, Christianity was used to sanctify slavery. And in more recent years, it has been used to bless war and even to justify atomic destruction of cities. There seems to be no end to our ingenuity when it comes to ways in which we try to make Christ weak like one of us. We Americans live in split-level houses; and we keep on trying to live a split-level existence: "In God we trust" and "In Arms we trust"; "This nation under God" and "This Nation as God." [20] But I do not believe God is going to let us go on this way. I think Dr. Paul Scherer was right when he said, "It's the face of God revealed to men in Jesus Christ that's brooding over this world, and it will not be shrugged off or spat upon and crowned with thorns any longer. There's no 'please' about it now; it's 'either,' 'or.' Either God and his will for you and me and all of us together, or civilization and democracy with it—is washed up. Civilization is in its last foxhole."

On the wall of my study, I have a painting which shows Jesus Christ standing alongside the United Nations building. He appears to be knocking at the door, waiting to be invited in, to be included in the councils of the nations. But there is no sign that he is going to receive any such invitation. I wonder how long we can exist; I wonder how long we can keep from destroying ourselves if we continue to keep him on the outside, if we continue either to ignore him altogether, or else to change his teachings and twist his words so that they seem to be approving everything we are doing? It is clear that he is just as strange, just as hard for us to understand today, as he was in the first century.

Perhaps it will always be that way. Perhaps that is God's way of keeping us humble and teachable. Perhaps God has given us the living Christ to be the eternally disturbing presence, the eternal stranger whom we can never fully know, whose demands we can never fully meet, so that we will always be fellow pilgrims with the Apostle Paul: "Forgetting the things that are behind and pressing on toward the goal for the prize of the upward call of God in Christ Jesus." (Philippians 3:13-14.) It seems to me that this is the "spirit of truth" which Jesus promised to his disciples. It is a *Holy* Spirit which comforts and strengthens, but the comfort comes only as we submit to its demands and bring our lives in harmony with God's purposes for them.

Winifred Kirkland wrote: "I did not choose this Presence in my life. In many ways, existence would be easier without it. If it were not for that incessant, ironic comment in my ear, it would be a simple matter to accept heard opinion, either religious or secular. Does that Presence make for quiet of the soul or disquiet? One thing only I know, Jesus is for me an unavoidable and constant challenge." And that is the way it ought to be. If we really stop to think, I'm sure we would not have it any other way.

Oh, there are times when it feels good to sing, "What a friend we have in Jesus. He walks with me, he talks with me, he tells me I am his own." There are times when we like to sail off into a beautiful dream world as the choir sings, "My God and I, we walk the fields together, we laugh and talk as good friends would and should." This makes us feel real good. It gives that sense of contentment and satisfaction which we dream about. But, God has wisely planned it in such a way that we cannot remain in that dream world. Just when we are ready to settle down and enjoy ourselves, there is a knock at the door. There is a disturbance at the gate. And no matter how hard we may try to ignore it, it persists. It will not go away. If we finally take a look to see who it is, there stands that stranger of Galilee, that man we thought we had left behind. He knocks at the door of our mystic sanctuaries. He knocks at the door of our ego-building testimony meetings. He knocks at the door of our protest meetings. He knocks at the gate of our racially segregated neighborhoods. He knocks at the top security gates of our military installations. He knocks for the sergeant-at-arms at the door of the U.S. Senate. He knocks at the door of the Corporation Board room. He knocks at the door of the Labor Union hall. He knocks at the door of the White House. He knocks at the door of our Seminaries. At these, and a thousand other doors, the stranger of Galilee knocks. Like the shepherd in search of the lost sheep, He will not give up. He will not go away.

I have struggled in this sermon. I try in every sermon to give a true picture of Jesus Christ; but no matter how hard I try, there always seems to be something beyond my words, something so elusive and so strange about him that I always realize I have failed to picture him as fully and as fairly as I should. Even as I proclaim him the eternal stranger, I know there is something more. Above the words," "I am not come to bring peace," I hear another voice saying, "Peace I leave with you. My peace I give unto you."

And then, I can only exclaim with Paul, "Who is sufficient for these things?" I can only join with him saying, "You must think of me as a signpost—that and nothing more. I can only point you to what I feel to be the greatest, the best, the most complete revelation of God's will for us that we can ever know." I can only say, "Come with me to Christ."

O God, forgive us that we have so often kept the door tight closed in Thy face. Give us the faith and the strength to trust the stranger of Galilee, so that He may truly become a part of our daily lives.

SUGGESTIONS FOR GROUP STUDY

Deal with the content of this sermon in detail to open this session. See the suggestions in the box on page 8 for some possible ways to do this.

Ask persons to work individually on this task, writing their responses or answers. What is the meaning of the writer's statement: "The more like us we picture Jesus as being, the less like Jesus we will have to be?" Can you state this idea in some other words? Illustrate the meaning of this idea by an example or experience.

Invite each member of the group who wishes to do so to share his or her responses to the above questions. Add other illustrations, examples, or experiences as they come to mind. Now discuss as a whole group: How can we come to understand Jesus as he really was—and is? How can we be sure we are not casting him in our own image or in an image comfortable and easy for us?

Focus now on a second statement of the writer's: "Perhaps God has given us the living Christ to be the eternally disturbing presence, the eternal stranger whom we can never fully know, whose demands we can never fully meet, so that we will always be fellow pilgrims . . ." In groups of three, discuss this statement in detail. Let one person in the triad indicate to another person in the triad why he or she agrees or disagrees with this statement. Let the third person in the triad listen carefully to the conversation, then report to the two persons what he or she heard as the two persons talked about this statement. Then rotate positions within the triad so that each person finally has an opportunity to explain his position with regard to this statement, to hear a position explained, and to observe and report on a conversation.

Allow time for triads to report any new insights or ideas to the whole group.

Conclude this session by sharing experiences of Jesus Christ knocking at the door of your community, your church, your family, or your own life. Describe for the group how you answered that call. Then pray aloud together the prayer printed at the end of this sermon.

V

MORAL LAW IS UNCHANGING

"The law of the Lord is perfect, reviving the soul; the testimony of the Lord is sure, making wise the simple." (Psalm 19:7, RSV.) "I am the way, the truth, and the life . . ." (John 14:6, TEV.)

As I continue trying to sum up what I believe to be the major truths of the Christian gospel, let me make a third affirmation. It is my firm belief that there is a divinely ordained moral law and that it is unchanging.

Adolf Hitler wrote in *Mein Kampf* that he would free the world of Mount Sinai, drive out of human conscience all thought of God's sovereignty, and substitute the sovereignty of the state. Thus, right would become what benefits the German state; wrong would be what does not benefit the German state. Lenin said to the Young Communist League in 1920, "We deny the fact that there is a moral law that comes to man from outside history." And Karl Marx suggested that they would not hesitate to revise the ten commandments, if such revisions were necessary to accomplish their goal.

Some anthropologists who have studied many different cultures and societies and have found wide differences in moral standards on such matters as sex relations, ownership of property, honesty, class and group relations, and other matters are saying there is no such thing as a universal principle of right and wrong. In the same way, there are some sociologists who tend to confuse *mores* and *morals*. As they research the trends and attitudes of our urban society, there is an increasing tendency to assume that whatever most people are doing and thinking is right. For instance, if a Gallup poll indicates that premarital sex relations seems to be a trend among young people, then they would say, "This may be a good thing after all." There are even some theologians who seem to be saying situations change and what is right in one situation may be wrong in another. There is really no basic moral law. In other words, there are many today who come out about where Lucille Ball, the television actress does. In a radio interview, I heard her say, "I judge everything by the question: Is this right for Lucy?"

In contrast, Christians have made three basic affirmations: First, there is a God who has created and who controls the universe. Second, he is the author of physical and moral laws which determine survival in his universe and which can be discovered and understood. Third, the moral law can best be understood by studying the life and teachings of Jesus Christ. This fact is summed up in Jesus' statement as quoted in John's gospel, "I am the way, the truth, and the life." This universal validity of God's law was also affirmed by the psalmist who wrote, "The law of the Lord is perfect, reviving the soul; the testimony of the Lord is sure, making wise the simple."

But even if you accept these basic affirmations, all your problems are not solved nor your difficulties dispelled. The real problems start when you try to apply these principles. So, let me first suggest some mistakes that many people have made.

First, they have said, "We'll find what is right by looking in the Bible, especially in the New Testament." Thus, the Bible is looked upon as being very much like the correct answer section that students turn to in the back of a mathematics textbook. All you have to do is find the right chapter and verse in the Bible and there you have your answer. This is a half-truth; and like most half-truths it is dangerous. It is true that the Bible is the greatest written source of ethical and moral wisdom we know anything about. It is an invaluable guide to which men need to turn

time and time again. We do believe that God speaks to
men through the Bible. He speaks as we read there about
various ethical and moral decisions men have made in the
past. He speaks as his prophets often point up the wrong-
ness of those decisions. And this sheds light on the decisions we have to make today, as we may face similar
circumstances. But, we do not always face similar
circumstances. There are many circumstances we face
today that were never faced by men and women of Bible
times. This was a problem even in Jesus' day. The Jews of
that day were trying to determine all their actions by the
laws of their Bible—the first five books of the Old Testament; but they found that many of those laws had to be
interpreted to fit different circumstances. The law said,
"Remember the Sabbath day to keep it holy." This meant
they were to do no work on the Sabbath; but what did
this mean? What was work and what wasn't? Well, the
scribes had drawn up elaborate definitions and classifica-
tions. It was not lawful to carry a load on the Sabbath,
so, they said, a man with a wooden leg could not walk. A
housewife could not do her housework on the Sabbath,
but she could tie on her apron, *provided* she could tie the
knot with one hand. These are the kinds of absurdities
you get into when you try to turn one book or one set of
laws into an absolute guide for all of life. And you will
remember that it was this literal legalism which Jesus
challenged. When sick people needed his help, he helped
them, whether it was on the Sabbath or not. He said, "the
Sabbath was made for man, not man for the Sabbath."
Thus, he was saying, "God expects us to put human life
and human need ahead of any law." In this and in other
ways, Jesus made it clear he believed God continued to
speak to men and to guide them; and that it is a mistake
to assume that all the answers are in a book.

In his Sermon on the Mount Jesus specifically challenged the literalists of his day, with the repeated words,
"It was said to you of old time . . . but I say unto you."
And he even tried to guard against the danger of his disciples turning his own words into a new law code. He kept
talking to them about the Holy Spirit or the Spirit of truth

who would guide them into further truth. John quotes him as saying, "I will pray the Father, and he will give you another Counselor . . . even the Spirit of truth . . ." (John 14:16-17, RSV.) "I have yet many things to say to you, but you cannot bear them now. When the spirit of truth comes, he will guide you into all the truth . . ." (John 16: 12-13, RSV.)

I believe Jesus would say the same thing to people today who insist that every ethical or moral decision must be made by quoting chapter and verse from the Bible. He would want us to use the Bible, as he did. He quoted from it to answer each of the temptations he faced in the wilderness and in numerous other instances throughout his life; but he did not let it become a barrier to new truths God might want to reveal to him. No rule in a book can be the end of it, no matter how good it may be. No rule can be the end of it, even if it is the "Golden Rule." No rule can provide a pigeonhole for every life-situation. You must always be prepared to go beyond the rule, as Jesus did, to the One who is the source of all rules. Ours is a living God and he can never be replaced by a dead set of rules. There may be times when we are ready to follow God's voice in going beyond the law, even as Jesus did when he dared to break the law about the Sabbath by healing men on that day. But, there will be other times when we will accept the great moral laws outlined in the Ten Commandments as the very bulwark of society, even as Jesus did. He told the rich young ruler that the first step toward discipleship was to keep the commandments. In the Sermon on the Mount, he said "Do not suppose that I have come to abolish the Law and the prophets; I did not come to abolish, but to complete . . . If any man therefore sets aside even the least of the Law's demands, and teaches others to do the same, he will have the lowest place in the kingdom of Heaven, whereas anyone who keeps the Law and teaches others so will stand high in the kingdom of Heaven." (Matthew 5:17-19, NEB.) So, when Jesus talked about living beyond the Law, he certainly did not mean disregarding the great moral laws or treating them as unimportant. He meant accepting the Law as a great gift from God—a key to happiness and right living. He would have joined with the psalmist in singing, "The law of the Lord is perfect, reviving the soul." But, he would also have insisted that the Law must never be accepted as a substitute for man's struggle to hear and to know what God is saying to him in every situation. The great moral laws which God has established and which are reflected in the Ten Commandments and in the Sermon on the Mount are much like the beacon lights which guide an airplane pilot. They serve as landmarks which help him to get his bearings; but he still needs to keep his radio on so he can listen to the radio signals and the directions from nearby control towers. So, we have these laws to serve as beacon lights; but we still must keep our hearts open to hear the more direct guidance God is prepared to give.

But, Jesus kept insisting that there is a higher law to which we must submit before we can ever find the blessedness or the happiness which he was talking about in the beatitudes. It might be called the unconditional imperative. It is the one thing which God demands of every one of us. Jesus was hinting at this when he said, "You must be perfect as your heavenly Father is perfect." A better translation might be to say, "You must be perfected—you must be completed as God created you to become. You must let nothing keep you from reaching your full potential." God's one purpose is not to squeeze you into some strange and uncomfortable mold. His purpose is for you to become what you potentially are—as one translator puts it: to "grow into complete maturity of godliness in mind and character." [21] This, then, is God's purpose for each one of us. It means that if I am to do what is right, I must do what God created me to do. I must be what God created me to be. So, God's will is not an arbitrary, external law laid down by a heavenly tyrant. It is not a strange law that demands our obedience. It is the silent voice of our own best self, our essential nature as it was first created by God. This, I believe, is what Jesus meant when he said God had sent him so men might have life and have it in all its fullness.

But, looking to Jesus as our guide sometimes leads to another mistake. It is the mistake of over-simplification. Some people have said, "We'll just face each situation with the question, "What would Jesus do?" At the turn of this century, Dr. Charles M. Sheldon, a Congregational minister of Topeka, Kansas, wrote a novel entitled, *In His Steps*. It became the best-selling book of that period; and has gone through some sixty printings since. It was the story of what happened when a newspaper editor and other persons in a city actually determined their actions by asking the key question: "What would Jesus do?" Of course, this is good as far as it goes; but we need to realize that there are some serious limitations on such an approach. On specific issues Jesus' situation was immensely different from our own. He was not confronted with many of the kinds of decisions that we face today. He did not have to decide whether to participate in international warfare, whether to produce or to use hydrogen bombs. He did not have to decide whether to keep on working for a firm that is engaged in unethical business practices or in the wasting or polluting of earth's resources. He did not have to decide whether to replace long-time, faithful employees with automated processes. Of course, the amazing thing is how much carry-over there actually is from Jesus' life and teachings to our modern problems. But it is a mistake to assume that you can always find a parallel and apply it. We have to realize that there are many situations where we need to remember Jesus' words, "His Spirit will guide you into all truth." Law—not even Jesus' words—must never be accepted as a substitute for man's struggle to hear and to know what God is saying to him in each situation.

A third dangerous mistake in this field of Christian decision-making is to say, "We'll let the church decide what is right or wrong." As you know, there were many in Jesus' day who said this. They simply accepted the standards and codes of conduct handed down by orthodox Judaism and as interpreted by the Scribes. But, as we have seen, Jesus challenged this comfortable philosophy. He insisted that each man is responsible to God for his own decisions, and that he must look to God's holy spirit to guide him, even as he guided Moses and Elijah and Jeremiah.

Today, there are a number of Christian churches which claim authority to make most major ethical decisions for their members. They insist that God has entrusted the Church as the body of Christ to be his spokesman; and so, men must look to the Church as their final authority on what is right and what is wrong. This appeals to a great many people. We are living in a topsy-turvy world; and it is increasingly difficult to know what we ought to do. So, many people are only too happy to turn this responsibility over to someone else. They want to be sure, at least, that they get to heaven; and so, they are eager to belong to a church which says, in effect, "If you will just obey our rules and observe our ritual, you can be sure of salvation."

Obviously, it can never be quite that simple. It is true that men need the guidance and the strength which can come from the Church. It has a long life, reaching back across the centuries, surviving the crises of many political, cultural, and theological conflicts. From the lessons of the past, from the example of saints and martyrs in earlier days, Christians today can and should gain insight and strength for the decisions they have to make. We need to study church history. We need to know how the great creeds were formulated, and why they are worded the way they are. But, we do not believe God is bound by the past. We believe that God most often speaks to men as they worship and work together in the church; but we know that he is forever seeking to reform the church and make it a better channel of his grace. As someone has said, "The church is always under judgment of the word whose duty it is to proclaim."

So, we come back to our original question: How can we know what is right? So far, I haven't been much help. I have rejected the answer of the relativists who say that we might as well not try to find absolute right or wrong, because there is no such thing. It changes with circumstances. I have said the Christian believes there is a divinely created moral law which can best be seen in the life and teachings of Jesus Christ. But, then, I have rejected the idea that we can find this moral law, just by looking in the Bible, or by setting out to imitate Jesus, or by depending entirely on Church decrees and codes. Then, what are we to do? How can we know what is right?

For answer, the Gospel does not offer some fool-proof and universal principle. Instead it offers the way of loyalty to a person. It says, "Look at Jesus Christ and you will see the essential structure of the moral universe—the way it works, the laws by which it is held together. *Follow him,* and you will find the way, the truth, and the life." Paul suggested that we are to "have the mind of Christ"; (I Corinthians 2:16, RSV.) and by this he meant we are to come to the place where we think as he thought. Someone told me once that when Bud Wilkinson was coaching his national champion Oklahoma football team, he used to arrange for his first string quarterback to be with him almost night-and-day. For as much time as possible, they ate together, played together, traveled together, studied plays together, until the quarterback got to the place he thought just as the Coach did. It is something like this which Paul had in mind when he suggested that Christians are to have the mind of Christ. We are to know his life and his teachings so well that they become a part of our own life. We don't keep asking, "What would Jesus do?" We do what he would do, simply because that is what seems to be natural and right.

But this brings us right back to the Bible, doesn't it? Especially the New Testament. We must live with it and read it so faithfully that we know much of it almost by heart. Here is God's way of bringing us close to the mind and the spirit of Christ. As Martin Luther said, "The Bible is the manger in which Christ lies," and it is only by turning to the Bible that we find him. Instead of looking to the Bible as a cold book of correct answers, we look to it as the place where we meet the living Christ and the God for whom he speaks.

This approach to the Bible will help us to avoid the sin of Pharisaism. This is the sinful attitude of the man who is so sure he is right that he assumes everyone else is wrong. So, if men think the Bible gives them the final and absolute answer to every question, they are going to become pharisaical. But if we think of the Bible primarily as the place where we can get better acquainted with a living Christ, we may not fall into this sin. When we stop to think, we know that there is no limit to your knowledge of a person. A person often does strange and unpredictable things. A hardened murderer becomes the bird man of Alcatraz; or a friendly neighbor and regular church-goer turns into an airplane highjacker. So it is with our knowledge of the living Christ—there is no limit to it. There is no time we can sit back and assume we know him so well that we have all the answers.

All we can do is commit ourselves to him, trusting in God's grace to keep us close to his mind and his spirit. We will stay close to the Bible. We will use the brain that God gave us to think as logically and as clearly as we possibly can, remembering that Jesus said we are to love God with our mind as well as with our heart. We will strive always to maintain an openness to the direction of God's spirit, remembering that Jesus said this spirit would guide us into all truth. We will seek guidance from all the creeds and the principles of the Church, realizing that they show us how others have faced similar problems; but also realizing that at this point of decision, we stand alone with God. With all the voices clamoring for attention, his voice may be hard to hear; but, for those who have learned how to listen; he has a clear and a living word.

An interpreter of one of Beethoven's great symphonies wrote, "At first the theme is distinct and clear. As the variations unfold, and the music gets more complicated, the theme is harder and harder to distinguish. Soon the music seems to have no direction or purpose whatever. But if one is already acquainted with the theme, he can hear it through all the apparent chaos, holding the music together, giving it direction and force." [22]

In Jesus Christ, God has given us the theme that holds the universe together. He has left it up to us to get well enough acquainted with that theme that we will be able to recognize it and follow it through all the apparent chaos which comes in a world where everyone seems to be trying to play his own tune and get up his own orchestra. Dr. Ralph Burhoe of the American Academy of Arts and Sciences wrote, "Man's continuity with the whole is bound by chains of cause and effect permeating all space and time. He is not a local transient accident . . . Every being and event is an inseparable part of the sacred whole . . . And the first corollary of this first law, man's kinship with his Creator, is man's kinship with all his fellow men, a kinship that is deeper than blood . . . We participate in a single, sacred whole, from which we are inseparable. Our gravest error is to put self first, to conceive of self in isolation." [23]

SUGGESTIONS FOR GROUP STUDY

Consider in detail the writer's ideas in this sermon; see the box on page 8 for suggestions for doing this.

In teams of four, discuss the process you follow for making decisions. Individually within the teams of four list in as much detail as possible the steps you go through in making a decision that involves a moral choice. Try especially to recall incidents in which you have had to make a choice between two apparently right alternatives or a choice between two apparently poor alternatives. How have you made your decisions in such cases? What elements or factors have you considered in such situations? Let the teams of four share insights from their discussions with the whole group.

Try conducting a number of "hearings": Seat three persons in front of the group. The task of these three persons is to present before the whole group, then defend before the whole group, the idea that the moral law is summed up in "I do what is best for me." These three persons should try to be as convincing as possible in their presentations of a case for this position. Other group members should make comments and ask questions of the three that challenge this position.

Next, select three other persons to present and defend

the case that the moral law can be discovered by following the words of the Bible exactly. Again, the remainder of the group should challenge, question, comment.

A third panel of three might appear before the group to present and defend the position that the moral law is summarized by "doing exactly what Jesus would do." Again, the rest of the group should challenge this position.

Finally, a panel of three persons might present the concept of moral law as they understand it as contained in this sermon. As with the other "hearings," the rest of the group should question, challenge, and seek clarification of this position.

(If time permits, other group members might defend other positions on the moral law, such as "what is best for the most persons," "what works best in accomplishing results," "what brings me the most happiness or comfort," "what the church says to do," and so on.)

After your series of at least four hearings, can you as a whole group prepare a consensus statement describing your understandings of the moral law?

Conclude this session by offering sentence prayers for understanding God's will, then sing together "O Come, and Dwell in Me," number 277 in *The Book of Hymns (The Methodist Hymnal)*.

VI

MAN DOES NOT SUFFER ALONE

"God shows his love for us in that while we were yet sinners Christ died for us." (Romans 5:8, RSV.)

At dusk on June 7, 1966 one of the largest and most destructive tornadoes ever recorded cut a half mile swath of death and destruction diagonally across the heart of Topeka, Kansas. The hospitals were packed with the injured. Late that night, as I was making my way in and around some of the victims in a hospital corridor, one of the nurses recognized me and called out, "Well, preacher, you ought to get a lot of converts out of this." "Yes," I said, "Either converts or atheists." She nodded in understanding, "Yes, I see what you mean."

Suffering which comes from such things as tornadoes and earthquakes will do one of two things: Either it will bring men closer to God, or it will turn them away from him, in bitterness and despair.

In view of the repeated tragedies which Job faced, ending with a tornado that killed all of his children, his wife exclaimed, "You must curse God, and die." At first, Job did just that. The account says, "Job opened his mouth and cursed the day of his birth." (Job 3:1, RSV.) In one of his plays, H. G. Wells has a character say, "If I thought there was an omnipotent God who looked down on battles and death . . . able to prevent these things . . . I would spit in his empty face."

But, there is another way of responding to tragedy and catastrophe. It is the way which comes to us from the world's greatest tragedy—the Cross of Jesus Christ. There you can see a man who faced as great a burden, as great a doubt as any of us have ever faced. It was no play acting when he cried out, "My God, my God why hast Thou forsaken me?" For a moment, it seemed that there was absolutely nothing left. Even the God who had been with him during his temptations in the wilderness, during the storm on the Sea of Galilee, when the mob tried to kill him in Nazareth, was gone. But then, there came a ray of light from out of the darkness, his despairing, grasping fingers felt the touch of another hand, and exclaimed, "Father, into Thy hands I commend my spirit."

There are mysteries here which we can never fully understand. But, there are also answers here which God wants us to understand. That is the reason he came to us in Jesus Christ. That is the reason he freely took upon himself the full flesh of a man, and faced the same tragedies and sufferings which we face. This was his way of saying, "I am one with you. I am always ready to provide a way out for you."

This is what the New Testament calls the Gospel or the "Good News." It is the good news that man does not suffer alone. The Apostle Paul summed it up when he wrote to the Christians in Rome, "God shows his love for us in that while we were yet sinners Christ died for us." A modern writer put it more bluntly when she wrote, "A number of years ago the Lord God announced to the men he had made, 'Here I am. If you want to kill me, go right ahead.' And they did." [24] And Soren Kierkegard, looked at the Cross above the altar of a church and wrote, "No matter what horror we have seen in the world, what horror there is of war, what horror there is of civil strife, or of sin, or evil, as we enter the house of God we face there a horror greater than anything man has ever seen. We face . . . the horrible fact that man crucified his God."

These are blunt ways to put it, but they helped me to come to a better understanding of what the good news is all about. You see, if Jesus Christ was who we say he was.

If he was God in the flesh, then when we sing about the good news of the Cross, we are singing about the good news of God's death. But, what is good about that? We often sing the great hymn, "Ask ye what great thing I know, that delights and stirs me so? . . . Jesus Christ, the crucified." Do we really mean that? Is there delight and joy in such a tragic event?

Peter and Paul and all the other New Testament authors and preachers insisted that there was. They believed in the resurrection and they found joy in it; but they also talked about the "good news of the Cross." What in the world did they mean?

Their meaning can be understood only in the light of what they believed about Jesus. Peter was the first to put it into words. That day at Caesarea Philippi, he said to Jesus, "You are the Christ, the son of the living God." (Matthew 16:16, RSV.) Paul put it more eloquently when he wrote, "God was in Christ reconciling the world unto himself." (2 Corinthians 5:19, RSV.) Now, if you can believe that—what the theologians call the doctrine of the Incarnation—then referring to the Cross as good news begins to make sense. If it is really true, as the book of Colossians says, "Christ is the visible likeness of the invisible God," (Colossians 1:15, TEV.) then what we see on the Cross and in the event leading up to the Cross is the most wonderful news in the world. It is good news about God.

The real question which most men ask about God is not, "Does he exist?" but "Does he care?" Most people believe in some kind of God. They don't question his existence but they do question his concern. On every hand, they see good people suffering; they see bad people prospering. They see little evidence that the meek are inheriting the earth; and so they have real doubts about the goodness of God. And at first, what happened on the Cross only seems to add more evidence, more reason for doubting that God cares. Jesus on the Cross seems to be saying, "Goodness does not pay. Virtue is not rewarded. For his kindness, Jesus got a crown of thorns; for his gentleness, he got a scourged back; for his love he got a cross too heavy to bear." From all the evidence, the wrong prevailed and God did nothing. But, look again. Think of what really happened.

If God were deeply concerned about man's suffering and sorrow, and if he wanted to make it clear to man that he was concerned, what could he do? Could he simply use his power to eliminate all suffering? Well, much of man's suffering comes because of what other men do or because of his own mistakes and sins. God could not eliminate this kind of suffering unless he took away man's freedom to choose and to act on his own. If he did that, man would be a robot or a slave, not a son of God. So, there must be some other way for God to show his concern and to help man face the sufferings of life.

It is this other way which is what the New Testament is all about. It is the way of a God who suffers with his children. It is the good news that the great God of the universe, the Creator of the stars and the atoms, actually became flesh and subjected himself to the vicissitudes of life on this earth. It is the good news that man does not suffer alone. Paul wrote, "he emptied himself, taking the form of a servant, being born in the likeness of men. And being found in human form he humbled himself and became obedient unto death, even death on a cross." (Philippians 2:7-8, RSV.) Similar statements are to be found throughout the New Testament. In a world which had long thought of God as being a distant and awful power, dwelling in unapproachable splendor, they were proclaiming the good news that God is not like this at all. God, instead of being wholly other than man, completely apart from him, is rather the boundless love who is wholly involved in, concerned about, the lives of his children. Paul and the other New Testament authors were saying, "He is one among us. When we suffer, he suffers. When we sin, we hurt him. If you don't believe it, just look at that man on the Cross. There you can see God's heart suffering." Paul summed it up, "If God is for us, who can be against us? He did not even keep back his own Son, but offered him for us all! He gave us his own Son—will he not also freely give us all things?" (Romans 8:32, TEV.) This was also the strengthening insight which came to Dietrich Bonhoeffer. He wrote from his cell in the Nazi prison, "God allows himself to be edged out of the world and onto the Cross. God is weak and powerless in the world, and that is exactly the way, the only way, in which he can be with us and help us. It is not by his omnipotence that Christ helps us, but by his weakness and suffering. . . . This is the decisive difference between Christianity and all religions. Man's religiosity makes him look in his distress to the power of God in the world. The Bible, however, directs him to the powerlessness and suffering of God. Only a suffering God can help." [25]

In one of Pearl Buck's books, she tells of two Chinese boys who were put into a Buddhist monastery by their parents to be trained as priests. But, later they ran away and joined the Communist army in North China. One of their first assignments was to destroy the churches in a certain area which had been taken over by the Communists. Late one evening they entered a small village chapel and started to destroy the images and pictures in it. Before they finished, it grew dark; so they decided to sleep there. As they were lying on the floor of the chapel, Kosen said to his friend, "Did you see the picture of the God nailed to a stick of wood?" Fahli answered, "Yes, what of it?" "Well, you know," Kosen said, "I never before saw a God who suffered."

In our churches we have sung about the Cross and talked about the Cross so much that we forget how daring and how different this picture of a God who suffers appears to those of other religions. As Paul wrote, it is "a message that is offensive to the Jews and nonsense to the Gentiles." (1 Corinthians 1:23, TEV.) But, in it we see the power of God and the wisdom of God. "For what seems to be God's foolishness is wiser than men's wisdom, and what seems to be God's weakness is stronger than men's strength." (I Corinthians 1:25, TEV.)

Dr. Albert Outler says, "the ground for our belief that the battle is worth our best is not that God is above it calling the shots, but that he is in it sharing the blows." [26] And Jesus on the Cross is the proof that this is not just wishful thinking. Here is God's pledge of what he has done and what he will be doing at all times and in all places. Just as the flash of the volcano reveals the fires that are always burning in the heart of the mountain, so what happened on Calvary shows the burning love and concern which is present in the God we serve.

In one of the European art galleries there is a painting of the Crucifixion. It pictures the Cross as being surrounded by what seems to be complete darkness; but, as you look closer, you can see far back in the shadows the dim outline of another Cross. This was the artist's way of saying what I am trying to say. If you look closely at Jesus' suffering on the Cross, you can see how much God suffers and how far he is willing to go in his love for men. You can see that he is not off somewhere calling the shots, but is in the thick of it with us sharing the blows. Piers Plowman exclaimed, "Who suffers more than God?"

But still we are tempted to point to the sin, the suffering, the pain in the world, and to ask, "Why? How can a God of love allow such things to be?" Sara Hay wrote:

> Because I heard His ways were just,
> In God's strong hands I placed my trust.
>
> I saw a child born lame and blind
> I saw a man of honest mind
> I saw his house despoiled and slain
> By thieves who lived to spoil again.
>
> I saw a woman's honor sold
> By her own lovely hand, for gold.
> She flourished to her life's soft close,
> While homely virtue starved and froze.
>
> I saw the meek, accepting dearth,
> Fall heir to some six feet of earth,
> But arrogance did not hesitate
> To claim the whole of man's estate.
>
> Charity furrowed his dry plain
> While on greed's acres fell God's rain
> Truth withered in a rocky cleft,
> With bay trees blossoming right and left.

I saw how red the rivers ran
Where man struck down his brother man.
Ten million murders brought to pass
All by the jawbone of an ass.

I found another verse, which read
More to my credence, for it said
Briefly, with less to rearrange
For faith's sad eye: "His ways are strange. . . ." [27]

Yes, these are the kinds of things that tempt us to exclaim, "It's clear that there is no good God in control of this world. If there were, He could not stand to see such things going on. He would do something about them." The New Testament replies, "He has done something about them. He has done the only thing the God and Father of Jesus Christ could do. He has done more than anyone has a right to expect him to do. He has actually joined in man's suffering. He has emptied himself and taken the form of a man in one supreme and final effort to save the world from those things that lead to such sin and suffering. There is nothing more that God could do without destroying man's freedom, and thus destroying man.

But, it is important to remember that this is not just something that God did some 1900 years ago on a rocky hill outside Jerusalem. As we have seen, the Cross is the picture of what God is doing all the time. Dr. Albert Outler wrote, "The Passion of Christ did not end at Golgotha: it goes on and on to the end of the world, wherever the passions of men go unredeemed. The sacrifice of Calvary is endlessly efficacious, not as a substitute for the sacrifices to which love calls us, but as a purgation of our sacrificial love from self-pity and bitterness. God-with-us (is what it means) God-with-us: in life's turmoils and drudgery, its vigils and sunbursts, unravelling and reweaving the strands of our memories and hopes, judging, thwarting, leaving us to suffer for our own misdeeds and those of others and yet never forsaking us even in our sufferings. God-with-us: not to dominate but to bless and yet also to prevent the final triumph of our resistance to his righteous rule. God-with-us: endlessly patient, endlessly concerned, endlessly resourceful. Here is the biblical secret of Emmanuel, the provident Mystery of God is 'present' in the very same projects to which he has assigned us, concerned above all that our experiences come to their created potential." [28]

But Jesus said we could not come to that "created potential" unless we are actually willing to take up our cross and follow him. Too often we quote Jesus' words, "Lo, I am with you always" without remembering that this was not an unconditional promise. These words were preceded by his command, "Go into all the world." (Matthew 28:20, 19.)

He had shown his disciples what he meant. He had gone out into the highways and the byways of Palestine. Where men were hungry, he fed them. Where they were troubled or sick, he comforted and healed them. Where they were caught in a vicious cycle of sin, he called them back to their better selves. Where they were oppressed by selfish economic or political forces, he stood with them in denouncing oppression and injustice. In these and many other ways, Jesus demonstrated how and where God wants us to work with him in building a better world. This is what Jesus meant when he said, "Go into all the world." This is what he meant when he said, "Take up your cross and follow me."

Is there any doubt in your mind about where we must go to follow this same Christ today? If it is true that he is still suffering and dying with the hungry, the poor, the oppressed, is it necessary for some preacher to tell you where they are, who they are? Is there any doubt what he means today when he says, "Take up your cross and come follow me? . . . Go into all the world?" And, is there any doubt that he will be with you on such a journey?

SUGGESTIONS FOR GROUP STUDY

As you have commenced the other sessions in this study, commence this session by seeking to understand exactly what the writer of this sermon is saying. Some suggestions for doing this are contained in the box on page 8.

Divide the group into four Bible study teams. Assign one of these Scripture passages to each of the four teams: John 9:1-7; Matthew 9:1-13; John 5:1-9; Mark 5:1-20. Ask each team to study its Scripture passage and to make a report to the whole group based on the following questions: What happened in this passage of Scripture? That is, retell this Scripture passage in your own words. What was the apparent cause of the suffering described in this passage? What was Jesus' attitude toward the suffering? Toward the person who suffered? How did Jesus respond to the suffering person? In what ways, if any, did Jesus 1) feel the suffering with the person? 2) seek to take the suffering upon himself? and 3) work to overcome the suffering and the pain for the person involved? Finally, what does this passage of Scripture say to you about suffering and our understanding of suffering?

As a whole group, can you make any statements about human suffering and God's role and response to suffering on which all members of the group can agree?

Test out some of our conclusions about suffering by role playing these situations:

• A mother whose three-year-old was run down and killed by a drunken driver asks you, "Why? Where was God?"

• A man sits at the bedside of his elderly mother, watching her slowly die as the result of a lingering but painful disease. He says, "Does she have to suffer this way?"

• A couple in your church school class, obviously distraught, blurt out, "Our daughter, the one in high school, is pregnant. What have we done, how have we failed, to have this happen to us—and to her?"

Allow time for discussion by the whole group following each role-play situation.

Conclude this session by sharing personal experiences of suffering and of finding strength or comfort through faith. They pray aloud together the Lord's Prayer.

VII

THE CHURCH IS GOD'S WAY

"You yourselves are our letter of recommendation, written on your hearts, to be known and read by all men; and you show that you are a letter from Christ delivered by us, written not with ink but with the Spirit of the living God, not on tablets of stone but on tablets of human hearts. (II Cor. 3:2-3. RSV.) "We have this treasure in earthen vessels . . ." (II Cor. 4:7, RSV.)

"It is God who organized both you and us into a Christian fellowship and gave us the power to endure. He put his stamp of approval on us and poured into our hearts the first install-ment of the Holy Spirit." (II Cor. 1:21.)

Will you use your imagination a bit? Go with me to visit the Christian church in Corinth in the year 51 A.D. Corinth was the fourth largest city in the Roman empire, with a population of over 700,000 people. Located on a narrow isthmus of land between the Aegean and Adriatic, it was the main port of call for most ships on their way from Asia Minor to Rome. Smaller ships were pulled the three and three-fourths miles overland across the isthmus on a kind of wooden railroad. Larger ships had their cargo un-loaded and transferred to sister ships on the other side. In the meantime, their crews spent their shore leave living it up in the city, where the temple of Aphrodite provided a thousand priestess-prostitutes and the shops along the south side of the city square provided plenty of oppor-tunity for drinking and gambling. In an age when public morality everywhere was at a low ebb, Corinth was no-torious for its lax morals. It had few long-time resident, because it was a new boom-city very much like San Francisco was in the gold-rush days. People were there from every part of the world; and its 500,000 slaves made human life seem cheap—made opulence and indulgence easy.

Coming into Corinth, we would probably arrive by ship from Ephesus. Then, we could walk up the main street from the harbor toward the Forum, until we came to the home of Gaius Crispus, a wealthy Roman merchant who had been converted by Paul and who made his large house available for church meetings. About sunset, after workmen were through their day's work, the members of the church began to gather. Roustabouts from the docks, slaves from the pottery and cloth factories, silver-smiths and carpenters, tent-makers, Jews, Greeks, Romans, Africans, come, each person or family carrying some food for the common meal. They are supposed to share their food, but you can see that the free citizens do not like to sit with the slaves, or the well-to-do with the poor. One group of friends has an abundant meal, while another group sits in a corner with little more than a piece of bread for each person. There are also some present who like the taste of wine and are not content with a sip or two. As a result, they become tipsy before the evening is over.

After supper, the leader calls the group to order and announces that he has just received a letter from Brother Paul. Eagerly, they gather round to hear the word from the founder of their church. He begins with kind words: "I am always thanking God for you. I thank him for all the enrichment that has come to you in Christ." But then, he starts dealing with some of their problems. He has heard that there is discord and divisions among them. He has heard reports of sexual immorality. He has heard that they are careless in associating with all kinds of immoral persons, some of them even continuing to patronize the temple prostitutes. He deals with each of these problems in a kindly but firm way, reminding them of their commitment to Jesus Christ. As we listen, we think about our own church in the twentieth century; and we find ourselves thinking, "Evidently these church members aren't too different from some that we know today. Their lives are a

THE CHURCH IS GOD'S WAY

long way from the principles they claim to follow." But
then, we are startled by these words of Paul, "You yourselves are our letter of recommendation, written on your
hearts, to be known and read by all men; and you show
that you are a letter from Christ delivered by us, written
not with ink but with the Spirit of the living God, not on
tablets of stone but on tablets of human hearts." He goes
on, "It is God who organized both you and us into a
Christian fellowship and gave us the power to endure. He
put his stamp of approval on us and poured into our hearts
the first installment of the Holy Spirit."

What in the world does he mean? How could this kind
of church represent Christ to the rest of the world? How
could God put his stamp of approval on such as these?
Weren't there some people around then, as there are now,
who said, "Don't ask me to be a Christian. Just look at
those people in the church. If that is what it means to be
a Christian, I don't want anything to do with the church."
Yes, I'm sure there were; and I'm sure Paul was very
much aware of them. Neither he nor other New Testament
writers dodge this fact. He wrote realistically about the
sins and shortcomings of church members; but still, he
addressed them as "those called to be saints in Corinth."
He called them a "letter from Christ" to the world. There
was no distinction between a visible and invisible church.
The local congregation thought of itself as the representa-
tive of the universal church. It was made to feel that, in
spite of its obvious weakness, it was the body of Christ—
the agent of God's redemptive work in the world. It was
a "letter from Christ." Paul did not say, "You *should* be a
letter from Christ," or "You *must become* a letter." He
said, "You *are* a letter from Christ." I think he would say
the same thing to any local congregation today. Every
local congregation, no matter how shallow its life together, nor how short-sighted its outreach, has buried
within it the treasure of Christ's presence. This is what
Paul meant as he wrote a bit later in the same letter, "We
have this treasure in earthen vessels."

Here we come to a point which is basic to our understanding of God. God does not speak through a vacuum.

He does not speak through some undefinable emanation which requires some specially prepared spiritual radar to be apprehended. He spoke most fully and most completely through Jesus Christ where, as John wrote, his word became flesh and dwelt among us. Here, we believe, is as much of God as can possibly be housed in human form. But here, also is the revelation of how God has spoken and how He would continue to speak. As the author of Hebrews put it, "In many and various ways God spoke of old to our fathers by the prophets; but in these last days he has spoken to us by a Son . . . He reflects the glory of God and bears the very stamp of his nature." (Hebrews 1:1, RSV.) Too many today assume that the church is just another cultural sociological phenomenon, with man as the initiator, the constructor, the preserver. But, the whole message of the Bible is that God is the initiator, the organizer, the preserver. He has done this in the most unlikely ways, through the most unlikely people. Any ground may be holy ground; any man may be a holy man. God spoke to Moses by a burning bush on a mountainside. He spoke to Isaiah in the Temple. He spoke to Elijah in the stillness that followed a mountain storm. He spoke to Paul on a busy highway. And then, the Bible also shows God speaking through all kinds of people—through a Jacob who got his start by cheating his own brother, through a Moses who could not control his temper, through a David who allowed lustful desire to turn him into a murderer, through a Peter who denied his Lord, through a Saul who led the attack on the first Christians.

Paul was steeped in this Biblical background; and so, he was able to make this daring statement to those delinquent, struggling new Christians in Corinth: "You are a letter from Christ . . . you are the body of Christ." He did not pretend the church was something it was not. With far greater realism than most modern preachers would dare to express, he wrote, "Remember, it has not been long since some of you were immoral, idolaters, adulterers, homosexuals, thieves, and drunkards. But you were washed, you were sanctified, you were justified in the name of the Lord Jesus Christ and in the Spirit of our God."

(I Corinthians 6:9-11.) Then Paul went on to deal with the specific sins and shortcomings of this congregation, making it clear he knew some of them were occasionally slipping back into their old ways—quarreling. drunkenness, licentiousness. But still he did not write them off as being useless to God. He believed that somehow God could use even such a church as that, and could make it a letter from Christ to a pagan society.

This is something which many critics of the church today have never learned. They demand a near-perfect Christian community, overlooking the fact that no church we read about in the New Testament meets that standard The New Testament never suggests that the church is or will become the perfect spokesman for God. Only Jesus Christ could be that. The church is the earthen vessel which keeps God's word in Christ alive and before the world.

Dietrich Bonhoeffer, the German pastor who was executed by the Nazis, saw this clearly. In his book *Life Together* he warned that self-appointed reformers and dreamers may be the greatest enemies of the true church. He wrote, "Every human wish dream that is injected into the Christian community is a hindrance to genuine community and must be banished if genuine community is to survive. He who loves his dream of a community more than the Christian community itself becomes a destroyer of the latter, even though his personal intentions may be ever so honest and earnest and sacrificial.

"God hates visionary dreaming; it makes the dreamer proud and pretentious. The man who fashions a visionary ideal of community demands that it be realized by God, by others, and by himself. He enters the community of Christians with his demands, sets up his own law, and judges the brethren and God himself accordingly. He stands adamant, a living reproach to all others in the circle of brethren. He acts as if *he* is the creator of the Christian community, as if *his* dream binds men together. When things do not go *his* way, he calls the effort a failure. When *his* ideal picture is destroyed, he sees the community going to smash. So he becomes, first an accuser of his brethren, then an accuser of God, and finally the despairing accuser of himself." [29]

This is the trap into which many twentieth century critics of the church have fallen. Bernanos, a French Christian of the nineteenth century, insisted that the church is like the farmer's wife on a typical European farm. A visitor to the farm might find things in great disarray: there are the workers to be given breakfast at five, the children to be awakened and fed for school, the farmer coming back to the house at nine for his full breakfast, the milk pails to be scalded, the big mid-day dinner to prepare, the children returning hungry at six, the darning to be done, the early bedtime so they can start again the next morning at five. The kitchen and farmyard seem in perpetual disarray. But, later, the visitor returns to the same farm. He finds the children crying. The farmer appears broken. The workers are quarreling. The yard is overgrown. The kitchen is chaotic. Why? Because the farmer's wife is dead. And so, said Bernanos, it would be this way for our world if we allowed the church, the bride of Christ, to die.

Of course, our real hope is the full assurance of the New Testament that God is always at work, reshaping and reaffirming the earthen vessel we call the church. Who could possibly have looked at that congregation in Corinth, or the one in Ephesus, or Rome, in Paul's day and have predicted that it would become a world religion? Who could look at the church of Europe in the 16th century, with its dissolute, money-grabbing leaders, and see any chance of it surviving, much less changing the political structure of Europe? Who could look at the empty churches and the foppish clergy of the Church of England in the 18th century and see any chance for Christianity to survive? But, what happened? God raised up a Polycarp and an Augustine in the early days. He called a Martin Luther in the sixteenth century and a John Wesley in the 18th, and through these men he did what many thought was impossible. He kept the body of Christ alive. It should be clear that it is not by our ingenuity that the reformation comes but by our obedient perception and reception of the new shapes God keeps preparing. God has given us a Gospel which keeps the church out-of-date, because we can never sit back and contentedly say to ourselves, "Now, this is what God wants." The minute we are tempted to do this, we see a man on a Cross. We hear a voice saying, "A new commandment I give you, that you love one another as I have loved you. . . . Come, follow me." And so it is, the church always finds itself puffing to catch up with what God calls it to be.

But, this call is not just something which came two thousand years ago or two hundred years ago. Ours is a living God, and his call—his reshaping hands are always present. As Jeremiah suggested we are like clay in the hands of a potter. God is always at work, always trying to produce better vessels, but still aware that they are earthen vessels and willing to make allowance for that fact. This is the only reason Paul could say to the Corinthian congregation, "You are a letter from Christ." This is the only reason it can be said to any Christian congregation today, "You, too, are a letter from Christ." With man it is impossible, but with God all things are possible.

Obviously, this does not mean that God uncritically places his stamp of approval on the church. Both He and all who love the church have a continuing "lovers quarrel" with it. The long history of Israel in the Bible and the history of the church since then, make it clear that God's purposes are often thwarted and his will denied by the hardness of men's hearts and the sinfulness of their desires. This, in fact, is the theme of the Bible. It is the story of God's effort to save a people and through them to save a world. It is the story of how, time after time, in spite of clear words from their prophets and the unmistakable signs of the times, they turned away from God and, as the Bible says, "did that which was not pleasing in his sight." But the Bible is also the amazing story of how, in spite of such actions, God continued to put up with them and kept trying to use them. It concludes with the unbelievable affirmation that God came down and entered into this sordid human scene as one of them; and even though they rejected him and hung him on a Cross, still he placed his trust in some of them, calling them to take his place as "the body of Christ" and saying to them "on this rock I will build my church, and the forces of death shall never overpower it." (Matthew 16:18, NEB.) Or, in the words of the author of First Peter, "you are a chosen race, a royal priesthood, a holy nation, God's own people, that you may declare the wonderful deeds of him who called you out of darkness into his marvelous light." (I Peter 2:9, RSV.)

Now, the most wonderful thing about all of this is the fact that you and I are still a part of that royal priesthood. The church first came into existence when Abraham heard God's call and obeyed. It exists today wherever men hear God's call and respond to it, even though their response may falter and even though they may misunderstand. God still can take their hunger and thirst after righteousness and can use it in building his Kingdom. In fact, the Bible makes it plain that this is his primary method of Kingdom-building.

On the other hand, it is not the church if it is simply a gathering of people who like to be with one another and who seek to accomplish their own goals and purposes. We do not gather in church primarily because we like one another. We do not gather because the church is a good place to meet nice people. We come to the church because we see God in Jesus Christ, and we seek to be with others who have made that same discovery. In our common loyalty to him, and in our common desire to serve him, we are drawn together very much as all kinds of insects are attracted by a light on a summer night. We come to church because Christ is the light of the world; and he has promised to meet us there.

Granted that there are times when the church seems to be a strange place to find Christ, even as that divided, quarreling, immoral mixture of people in the church in Corinth seemed to be, still it is in and through the church that Christ can and must speak to the world. In some strange and mysterious way, God has ordained that the church is to be a letter from Christ to the world he loves and seeks to redeem. Here is the extension or expansion of the Incarnation. Paul wrote that God "was revealed in human shape." The word became flesh, and the treasure was placed in earthen vessels. We cannot get away from some kind of human structure and organization. This is just the way God speaks and acts in our world. But these structures need constantly to be changing. The church and its members must always live in the tension of the old order yielding to the new, letting go the obsolete, holding fast to that which is good, and reaching out to that which is better. The church is sometimes petty. It gets mechanical and forgets what it is. It goes through the motions but there is no life. But, still, it is here in the church that men come together, Sunday after Sunday, to be confronted and comforted by the Gospel—the only thing that can save us and save the world. This is the recreative power which is always present in this husk we call the church; and as long as we expose ourselves to it, just so long will God keep performing miracles and turning us into something we can never be in our own power. He will actually make us a letter from Christ. He did it in first century Corinth. He can do it in twentieth century Chicago or Houston or Los Angeles.

SUGGESTIONS FOR GROUP STUDY

Commence this session by focusing on the writer's ideas contained in this sermon. The box on page 8 contains some suggestions for doing this.

Ask each person to write completions for these sentence stems:

To me the church is_____.

I look to the church for_____and I need the church for_____.

The biggest problem with the church as I see it is _____.

If I could change one thing here in our own church, I would_____.

I believe God is calling our church to_____.

In teams of three, share completed sentences. Then, working in teams of three, using your own ideas and the ideas contained in this sermon, prepare a one-para-graph definition of the church. You might want to com-mence your definition with this sentence stem: The church is intended by God to be_____. Work also in the teams of three in determining how your own local church can become more like the church as God intends the church to be. Cite some specific activities your church could undertake to become more what you con-sider the church should be.

Let teams of three share their discussions and ideas with the whole group. How were the teams' definitions of the church similar? How were they different? How do you account for any differences? What factors or characteris-tics were common to all the definitions?

As a whole group, discuss this sentence from this ser-mon: "God has given us a Gospel which keeps the church out-of-date." What does this statement mean to you? What does it mean to your church? What does it mean to your participation within your church? How can your church recognize and know the direction in which God wants it to move? Why should your church try to keep up-to-date if God has given the church a Gospel which keeps it out-of-date? What, specifically can your church do to become more "up-to-date" in terms of the Gospel?

Read aloud together the first paragraph of The Order for Confirmation and Reception in to the Church, number 829 in The Book of Hymns (The Methodist Hymnal). How does this statement correspond with your understanding of the definitions of the church? How did you feel when you first heard this statement as you were received into the church?

Close this session by affirming one another as members of the church in any way that seems appropriate. This might be through a word, a gesture, an expression, or an activity.

VIII

CONVERSION IS IMPORTANT

"Except ye be converted, and become as little children, ye shall not enter into the kingdom of heaven." (Matthew 18:3, KJV.) "Unless one is born anew, he cannot see the kingdom of God." (John 3:3, (RSV.)

For several chapters now we've been thinking together about the major points of the Christian gospel. But this will be little more than an intellectual game unless it leads to a commitment to the Christ who embodies these truths. It's all very well for you to read what the preacher says he believes; but it's not going to make one bit of difference unless you respond—unless you say, "Here is where I stand!"

This is the reason Jesus rode into Jerusalem on a donkey instead of a war horse. This was his way of calling upon men to take a stand with him for the way of peace and goodwill and justice. This was his way of saying, "I cannot be neutral nor can you. Here is where I stand! If you believe the things I have been teaching, then you must deny yourself and come follow me."

In Greek mythology, Proteus was a God who was able to change his shape with great ease. He could change from wild boar to lion to dragon to man whenever he desired. But, one thing he refused to do; he would not commit himself to any single form. You could never be sure just who or what he was going to be.

I don't need to tell you there are many people who are
often shifting from one stance to another. In one place,
they are this kind of person. In another place, they are a
different kind of person. You can never be sure what to
expect from them.

To me, this is the height of phoniness and hypocrisy,
but some seem to feel this is the only way to get along.
Dr. Robert Lifton, Professor of Psychiatry at Yale University wrote an article for the Yale Alumni magazine entitled
"Protean Man." He took the position that this kind of
shifting, changing stance may be the way to mental health
in our time. He illustrated what he meant by quoting from
one of his patients, a young school teacher, who said, "I
have an extraordinary number of masks I can put on or
take off. The question: Is there or should there be, one
face which should be authentic? I'm not sure that there is
one for me. I cannot imagine a single act that I could not
commit." [30] He went on to compare himself to an actor
on the stage who performs any number of different roles,
equally well.

Dr. Lifton then wrote, "I would stress that this protean
style of life is by no means pathological, and in fact may
well be one of the central adaptive patterns of our day."
In other words, there is nothing to be concerned about if
a man does not have an integrating, unifying purpose for
his life. If he shifts from one life-style to another, as easily
as a man might change his suits, or an actor might change
his roles, there is nothing to worry about. "Don't sweat
it," as they say. When in Rome, do as the Romans do.

Dr. Lifton concludes, "Until relatively recently, no more
than one major ideological switch was likely to occur in a
lifetime, and that one would be long remembered as a
significant individual turning-point, accompanied by pro-
found soul-searching and conflict." But today "it is not
unusual to encounter several such shifts, accomplished
relatively painlessly, within a year or even a month. . . .
The rarity is a man who has gone through life holding
firmly to a single ideological vision."

Now, if this psychiatrist is right, then the whole idea of
conversion which we Christians have emphasized is

wrong. It is out-of-date; and it would be a sure sign of maladjustment to say with Paul, "For me to live is Christ . . . It is no longer I who lives but Christ who lives in me . . . Not that I have already obtained this or am already perfect; but I press on to make it my own, because Christ Jesus has made me his own." (Philippians 3:12.) If Dr. Lifton was right, then Jesus was maladjusted when he said, "My will—my one purpose—is to do the will of Him who sent me . . . I must be about my Father's business." And he was leading men astray when he said, "You must be born again . . . Seek first the kingdom of God and his righteousness . . . Deny yourself, take up your cross, come follow me." In another place he said, "Except ye be converted, and become as little children, ye shall not enter into the kingdom of heaven." (Matthew 18:3, KJV.)

There has been much misunderstanding and misinterpretation of these words of Jesus. They have been used by some to pass judgment on others. They have caused many to carry unhealthy guilt feelings because they couldn't claim to have the kind of experience some insisted they must have. And this has led some psychiatrists to take the kind of position affirmed by Dr. Lifton. But, I believe Jesus' words have been grossly misunderstood and misinterpreted. I heard about a zealous evangelist who was driving down a country road. He saw a farmer plowing in a field alongside the road; so, he stopped his car, got out, and waited until the farmer came to the end of the row next to the fence. After they had exchanged greetings, the evangelist said, "My brother, are you a Christian?" The old farmer said, "No, the Christian Brothers live down the road about three miles. My name is Smith." "Oh no," said the evangelist, "That is not what I mean. Do you know that you may be lost?" "Naw!" said the farmer, "You can't kid me. I've lived right here for twenty-five years, and I sure ain't lost." Frustrated, the evangelist tried again, "My friend, you don't understand what I'm saying. What I want to know is: Are you ready for the Judgment Day?" "When is that?" said the farmer. "Well, sir," the evangelist replied, "Nobody knows for sure. It may be today. It may be tomorrow." "Oh," said the farmer, "For goodness sake, don't tell my wife. She'll want to go both days."

If we are going to avoid this kind of misunderstanding and misinterpretation, we must try to find out just what Jesus and the New Testament writers meant when they talked about "conversion." The Greek word which is translated "be converted" is a verb which literally means to turn around; so the Revised Standard translation reads, "unless you turn and become like children, you will never enter the kingdom of heaven." Jesus evidently had a characteristic habit of swinging around and looking at people. For instance, Luke says that when Peter was denying that he even knew Jesus, after the arrest in the garden, "the Lord turned and looked at Peter." (Luke 22:6, RSV.) In another instance, the Gospel of John says that outside the garden tomb, "Mary turned around and saw Jesus." (John 20:14, NEB.) The Greek word which is used in both instances is the same word which is also translated "be converted." So Dr. William Barclay has written a book on Christian conversion which he titles, *Turning To God.*

But, Jesus and the New Testament make it clear that this is not something which one can do on his own initiative alone. To the wise teacher, Nicodemus, who was used to thinking things through and working things out for himself, Jesus said this experience of new birth is as much beyond your control as the blowing of the wind. To his twelve disciples, Jesus said, "You did not choose me: I chose you." (John 15:16, NEB.) In fact, the whole Bible is not the story of good persons turning to God. It is the story of a good God who seeks persons like a persistent "hound of heaven" and keeps after them until they are stopped and turned around. The Bible understands that most individuals are indifferent to God until they face some real crisis or danger; and then, they get "foxhole religion." It understands that many deliberately evade God because in the words of John's gospel, "they love darkness rather than light." (John 3:19, TEV.) They don't want to turn around and stop what they are doing. On the other hand, there are those who give lip service. They acknowledge the existence of God, but they keep him on the circumference of life. They are like the brilliant Voltaire who said of his relation with God, "We nod, but do not speak."

The one dominant characteristic of all these attitudes is that the person's own desires, ambitions, feelings are at the center and dominate everything. Like Dr. Lifton's young school teacher, the primary question is: "What mask can I wear so I can get happiness for myself?" So, what Jesus was saying when he talked about conversion was that a man must be permanently turned in the direction of God rather than himself. God's will must take the place of his own selfish will. Or, to put it another way, in real conversion, a man is turned around and left permanently facing God. The new Dutch Catholic catechism says, "To be lost means to be closed in on oneself, without contact with others or with God." So, to be converted—to be saved—means to be turned outside oneself, toward others and toward God.

But, no man can do this on his own; no matter how hard he tries. Dr. Albert Einstein once wrote, "It is easier to denature plutonium than to denature the evil spirit in man." This was one of the central themes in the writings of Dr. Reinhold Niebuhr. He kept insisting that even good men with the best of motives usually end up in sinful situations unless they are saved by a Divine power from beyond themselves. So, Jesus said, "You must become like children—you must lean upon a heavenly Father even as our children lean upon us.

This turning to God, trusting in God, can come only as persons turn away from other things. Jesus said, "You cannot serve God and mammon." (Matthew 6:24, RSV.) He called men to seek first the kingdom of God and his righteousness. Jesus knew that a man's god is that to which he gives his life, that for which he has ultimate concern. Paul wrote of those who are lost because "their god is the belly," or "their bodily desires." (Philippians 3:19, RSV, TEV.) And he spoke of conversion as "turning away from those idols, to serve a living and true God." (I Thessalonians 1:9, RSV.) So, the New Testament makes it clear that being converted means turning away from an obsessive concern for money and for bodily indulgences. It does call for a clear commitment to self-sacrifice and service. Jesus was called a glutton and a winebibber by the ascetics of his day because he enjoyed the feasts and the parties of the common people and because he found so much joy in life. On the other hand, the rich young ruler, Nicodemus, and others turned away because Jesus' way called for too much sacrifice. So, being converted to Jesus' way evidently means being able to have a healthy, uncluttered outlook on life. In fact the Greek New Testament word "soteria" which we translate "salvation" was originally not a religious word at all. It means quite simply, "health and well-being." In a Greek papyrus letter of that day, a soldier named Apion wrote to his father Epimachus, "I beg you to send me a few lines about your soteria." [31] In other words, tell me how you are. So you could say, "To be saved means to have a healthy life." Jesus said, "I am come that they might have life, and that they might have it more abundantly." (John 10:10, RSV.) But he still insisted that this could come only through conversion— only by turning away from those things that destroy and turning to those things that give life.

I heard, at a lecture at Baker University in October 1968, one of the world's great psychiatrists, Dr. Victor Frankl, say that a lack of purpose, a failure to have some real commitment beyond oneself, is one of the greatest reasons for neurosis in our time. He calls this the "noogenic" neurosis, from the Greek word "noos" which can be translated as "mind" or "meaning" or "purpose." So, he said, failure to have such a unifying purpose causes neurosis.

You may remember that during World War II, Dr. Frankl was imprisoned in a Nazi concentration camp. As he and his fellow prisoners struggled to maintain their sanity and to stay alive, he noticed that some of the prisoners would stop struggling, give up hope and die, while others, in the same situation, had the fortitude to stick it out. As a psychiatrist, he kept asking, "Why? What makes the difference?" He came to the conclusion that the difference lay in the fact that some had a definite purpose, something to which they had committed themselves, while others had no such purpose. Those who had the purpose, the commitment, were the ones who survived.

Thus, he decided that the major role of a psychiatrist is to help his patient find that unifying, worthwhile purpose to which he can commit his life. He calls this theory of psychiatric treatment: logotherapy. And he says, "What a man is, he has become through that cause which he has made his own." This means that the Apostle Paul became the truly integrated man when he was able to say, "For to me to live is Christ . . . I am crucified with Christ." (Philippians 1:21, RSV.) When he stopped trying to save himself and started working with Christ to save and help others, there came a poise, a strength, an inner joy which nothing could destroy. He discovered what Jesus meant when he said, "Whoever loses his life for my sake will find it." And this great change which came in Paul's life is what the Christian Church has meant when it has talked about the need for conversion, regeneration, re-birth.

But, this turning can come for different people in different ways. Too many people have tried to standardize conversion. Some have tried to make Paul's experience on the road to Damascus the norm. They have insisted that unless there is a blinding, shocking, voice-from-the-sky experience it cannot be called conversion. But, the New Testament makes it clear that not all those who were converted to Christ's way started in this way. There were just as many like Peter and Matthew or Martha and Mary who turned and started walking with Jesus in a quiet way. They began with him, not fully knowing what the end would be. But, the important thing was the beginning, or the turning. John Wesley wrote, "It is not necessary to be able to pinpoint a moment in one's life as the moment of salvation, but it is essential that a Christian be able to say with Paul, 'I am being saved.' "

This is not to say that a highly emotional conversion experience may not be as good as a more gradual one, or vice versa. In most cases where life is really at stake, our emotions are deeply involved. John Wesley described his own conversion as a heart-warming, deeply moving expe-

rience; but those around him in the Aldersgate prayer
meeting probably didn't realize how much his life had
been changed. On the other hand, there were many of the
miners and factory workers to whom Wesley preached
who were so deeply moved that they responded with
shouting and tears. Conversion affects different people in
different ways; and to insist that my way is the only way
is like trying to tell the wind of God's Spirit which way to
blow. Jesus warned Nicodemus, "The wind of God's saving spirit blows wherever and however it wishes." (John
3:8.)

Another important thing to remember about the New
Testament definition of conversion is that it was interpreted as only a point of beginning, not the ultimate experience of a Christian's life. If, as Jesus suggested, we are
to turn and become like children, then, obviously we are
to grow as children grow. Jesus did not say, "Come, be with
me." He said, "Come, follow me—come walk with me."
He said "I will make you fishers of men." (Mark 1:17,
RSV.) And the account in the Gospels as well as the Book
of Acts is the story of the many ups and downs in that
"making" process. When these first disciples turned to
Jesus, they were not so changed that they did not need
much more changing and growing. All the ups and downs
of Peter's life are typical of many others who were converted.

There are some today who think of conversion as a
once-for-all experience and who often talk about the day
of Pentecost when three thousand people were converted
and baptized. But if you will read Acts 2:42 you will find
the writer saying about these converts, "They devoted
themselves to the apostles' teaching and fellowship, to the
breaking of bread and the prayers." In other words, they
devoted themselves to a continuous effort to learn more
about the faith. They did not feel finished off by their
conversion experience; rather, they felt God had turned
them around and started them on a new journey.

So, conversion not only meant turning to God; it not only
meant turning away from things that are ungodly; it also
meant turning to an experience of fellowship and learning

in the church. There is always a danger of assuming that conversion is primarily an individual matter in which a person is concerned only with saving his own soul. Of course, there is a sense in which it must be a highly individual matter. At the point of decision—at the point where Christ looks you in the eye and says, "Come, follow me," you are the only one who can make that answer. No one else can do it for you. But when you answer, "Yes," when you turn and start walking with him, at that point individualistic religion ends.

The real test of any individual's conversion is the extent to which it unites him with his fellow-men as well as with God. It is very significant that in the New Testament the pictures which describe the Christian life are what might be called "group pictures." There is the picture of the sheep and the flock (John 10:15); the human body and all its parts (I Corinthians 12:12); the house and the stones in its walls (I Peter 2:5; Ephesians 2:21). It seems clear that for the first Christians being converted meant moving into a life of togetherness with others who had had the same experience and had made the same commitment. Being in Christ meant being a part of his body, the church. This was not even debated. It was assumed.

For fifteen years, I chaired a television panel of ministers which received telephone questions from viewers. One of the most frequent questions was: "Does a man have to join a church in order to be a Christian?" In the early days of the Christian church, such a question never occurred to men. They believed that Jesus had gathered his disciples into a group for a purpose. They believed that they were called together as "God's people" so they might continue the covenant he had made with Israel. This they felt was something they had to do as a group—something they could not do as separate individuals. They would heartily have agreed with John Wesley when he wrote, "No man ever went to heaven alone." What is more, no man is truly converted unless he feels compelled to belong to the group Jesus referred to as "my little flock," but which is now called the Church of Jesus Christ.

There is one thing more about Christian conversion which is made clear by the New Testament. It suggests that conversion not only means turning to God, turning away from ungodly things, turning to the church; it also means turning to the world with a new sense of compassion and concern. The fellowship into which the convert entered was something which led to practical, costly, and sacrificial aid to those who were in need out in the world. This is made especially clear by the Book of Acts. It describes the first church as a group whose primary concern was to minister to those who were in need and to bring healing to those who were sick. In the fourth chapter of Acts we read, "there was not a needy person among them, for as many as were possessors of lands or houses sold them, and brought the proceeds . . . and laid it at the apostle's feet; and distribution was made to each as any had need." And, James writing about the same time said, "Suppose there are brothers or sisters who need clothes and don't have enough to eat. What good is there in your saying to them, 'God bless you! Keep warm and eat well!'—if you don't give them the necessities of life?" (James 2:15-16, TEV.) I'm sure they had heard and taken seriously Jesus' words, "Whenever you refused to help one of these least important ones, you refused to help me." (Matthew 25:45, TEV.)

It seems to be the plain teaching of the New Testament that the so-called "do-gooder," the "social gospeler," is more nearly fulfilling God's will than the cloistered saint absorbed in his prayers and his Bible. For the first Christian, the words "God so loved the world" meant he expected them to love it too—love it enough that they worked together to change it and make it better. They very seriously thought of themselves and of their church as being agents of change. They knew the social structures of the world were a long way from what God wanted, and so they joined hands in working to change them for the better. So much so, that Luke says they were referred to "as those who have turned the world upside down." (Acts 17:6, RSV.) When the Christian was converted and turned to God, he felt compelled to do everything he could to turn the world to God.

And it was all done with the joyous abandon of men and women who felt they had been given a new lease on life. They were social reformers, but they were not the long-faced, holier-than-thou persons who so often associate with reforms. Jesus once described this new life as being like the joy of a poor laborer ploughing a field. His plough suddenly uncovered a buried treasure. He rushed home excitedly, told his wife the great good news, and started selling everything he had so he could buy that field.

The Book of Acts is filled with this kind of excited joy. Outsiders sometimes accused the new converts of being drunk because of their exuberance. But that is the way it always is when a person truly turns to God. It is Paul in the first century exclaiming, "I know that in everything God works for good with those who love him . . . Thanks be to God who gives us the victory through our Lord Jesus Christ." It is John Wesley in the 18th century: "I felt my heart strangely warmed . . . An assurance was given me that he has taken away my sins, even mine." It is the teen-age drug user described in a TIME magazine article who had been suffering from recurring drug trips and who had been saved from this compulsion, shouting, "My flashbacks are gone!"

Yes, conversion still makes a difference. Conversion is still important. It brings a joy and a strength which is the very essence of life itself. As William Tyndale wrote in the preface to the first English New Testament, "Here is good, mery, glad and joyful tydings, that maketh a manes hert glad, and maketh hym synge, daunce and leepe for joye."

SUGGESTIONS FOR GROUP STUDY

See the suggestions in the box on page 8 for dealing with the contents of this sermon. Follow one or several of these suggestions to be sure that all group members understand the writer's ideas.

Let each person in turn describe a personal experience

of a major change in stance, belief, understanding, or opinion. Some persons will want to describe religious conversion experiences. But as not all persons have had experiences that they comfortably could call conversions, focus instead on any experiences of drastic changes in outlook or attitude. Ask each person to describe such an experience, then to indicate the factors that caused that experience. What role did other persons play in this experience? How much of this radical change was due to factors beyond the individual's control? To factors over which the individual had some control? To what extent was this change the result of a process that had been developing for some time?

One member of the group might be listing factors that seem common to all these experiences as the experiences are related. When everyone has shared an experience, post this list of factors on chalkboard or newsprint. How do your experiences of conversion and radical change and the factors which cause such changes compare with the experiences of Christians such as Paul, Augustine, Luther, Wesley, and others?

As a whole group, discuss this question: Must an individual experience a conversion before he or she can become a Christian?   Realize that to answer this question, your group will need to come to some understanding of the words "conversion" and "Christian."

Ask each person to write a completion for this sentence stem: Conversion is not the end but the beginning because _____. Share your completed sentences, then discuss as a whole group this question: If conversion is not an end but a beginning, what follows conversion?

Finally, consider this question: How can our church help persons understand the nature and necessity of conversion?

End this session with a period of silent prayer, then read aloud together "God So Loved the World," number 648 in The Book of Hymns (The Methodist Hymnal).

IX

THERE IS HOPE

"Blessed be the God and Father of our Lord Jesus Christ! By his great mercy we have been born anew to a living hope through the resurrection of Jesus Christ from the dead." (I Peter 1:3, RSV.)

Throughout this book we have been thinking together about the major points of the Christian Gospel. In this chapter, we come to the most important point of all. It is the affirmation that there is hope!

This hope is symbolized by Easter. Easter is the happiest day of the Christian year. This is a time for joy and celebration. It is a time for singing and laughter. So, in some churches the ritual for Easter day calls for the priest to lead the congregation in a period of "Holy Laughter." But if you are to understand the celebration of Easter you need to recall the most desperate, the most lonely the most tragic situation you have ever faced in your life. You must try to feel what that man on the cross felt when he exclaimed, "My God, my God why hast Thou forsaken men?" You must try to put yourself into the shoes of the first apostles, hiding in a secret room, on a back street, in the city of Jerusalem. The doors are bolted; the windows are covered. There is only a single, flickering oil lamp. It gives enough light to enable them to see each other; but not enough to shine through any cracks in the doors or windows. They are talking in hushed whispers, as men often do in countries under totalitarian rule. They are talking about the leader of their group who has just been arrested and executed by those totalitarian rulers. They are wondering how they can keep from meeting the same fate. But their conversation is strained and limited. Each man seems deep in his own thoughts, and there is very little real sharing of thought or plans. Each one seems afraid to talk, because he remembers that another member of their group, one they had all trusted, had been the very one who betrayed their leader to the authorities. They are afraid to trust anyone; and so they sit there in the semi-darkness of that room, munching listlessly at some of the food on the table, talking some; but mostly just sitting in silence, afraid to talk, afraid to leave their hide-out; expecting at any moment to hear the knock of a mailed fist and the command, "Open in the name of the Emperor." They were completely and utterly demoralized and disillusioned. The one they had believed to be the Messiah, the Deliverer of their people, had been rejected by their religious leaders and crucified by the Romans.

Have you ever felt that God had completely deserted you? Have you ever felt there was no use trying to be good or decent or honest? Have you ever felt as Carlyle did when he wrote, "God sits up in heaven and does nothing"? A few years ago, Tennessee Williams, the play writer, said to a TIME magazine reporter, "There is a horror in things, a horror at the heart of the meaninglessness of existence . . . It seems the cards are stacked against us. The only victory is how we take it." Mathematician Norbert Wiener wrote, "In a very real sense we are shipwrecked passengers on a doomed planet."

If you can understand these feelings, if you can know the utmost depths of human despair, then you are ready to hear the good news of Easter. If you have wept at the foot of the Cross on Good Friday then, and only then, are you truly ready to sing "Hallelujah" on Easter Sunday. This is the only way you can fully know what the Easter sermon is about when it says that the life, the death, and the resurrection of Jesus Christ are our hope. This is the only way you can understand what the Apostle Peter was

talking about when later, in the midst of intense persecu-
tions, he wrote, "Blessed be the God and Father of our
Lord Jesus Christ! By his great mercy we have been born
anew to a living hope through the resurrection of Jesus
Christ from the dead." This living hope can be seen in
three ways: It can be seen in a man on a Cross. It can be
seen in an empty tomb. It can be seen in a living Christ
who walks by men's sides so that their hearts burn within
them at the joy and strength of his presence.

First, God's answer to man's despair can be seen as
God became a part of that despair through Jesus' death on
the Cross. As we saw in the fourth chapter of this book,
if you want to see what God is doing about man's inhu-
manity to man, if you want to see what he is doing about
all the suffering and pain and trouble that men must face,
look at Jesus on the Cross. Or, sit down some evening
and read through any one of the Gospels. Read the life-
story of this man of sorrows, who was acquainted with
grief. Stand with him on the Mount of Temptation and see
how he faced the same temptations you face. Walk with
him as he steadfastly set his face to go to Jerusalem, even
though this probably meant torture and death. Wait quietly
under a gnarled olive tree and listen to the agonizing
prayer of a young man who had so much for which to
live but knew he had to die. Watch in shame as one of his
closest friends betrays him with a kiss. Note the hollow
mockery of justice as he is condemned to death by the
highest and best courts of his day. Hear the cruel whistle
and thud of the lash as he is prepared for his execution.
Walk the Via Delorosa and watch as he is forced to carry
his own cross. Listen to the blows of the hammers as the
soldiers drive the spikes into the tender nerves of his
hands and his feet. And then, if you are able, watch the
sight which often made strong men faint. Watch the con-
vulsive, uncontrollable muscle spasms of a strong man
who is being forced to die by degrees. Hear that most
human of all cries, "My God, why?" Hear that most divine
of all prayers, "Father, forgive them . . ." Try to understand what he meant when he sighed, "It is finished."

If you will do this, with the eyes of your imagination

wide open, you can begin to understand what Paul meant when he wrote, "God was in Christ." You can begin to see what theologians have meant when they have insisted that in Jesus' life and in his death on the Cross we have been given a picture of what God has done and is doing through all time and eternity. Here is God's heart suffering in public. Instead of sitting in heaven doing nothing, we see that He is here in our midst, bearing our griefs and carrying our sorrows.

But, there is even more to God's answer than this. There is not only the answer which is symbolized by the Cross. There is also the answer which is symbolized by the empty tomb. Here is God's answer to those who feel that evil and falsehood and wrong always seem to have the last word over goodness and truth and right. At the end of the day, when they took that lifeless body down from the Cross, when they carried it to a tomb which was carved in the solid rock, when they rolled the heavy stone across the entrance and placed a Roman seal on it, everyone concerned was convinced that this was the end. Upon this point, both friend and foe would have agreed. There was no use pretending any longer. Goodness had done its best. Evil had won. It was the same old story repeated again. For a few brief months, Peter and James and John along with Mary and Martha and the others had dared to dream that it might be different. They had dared to believe that God was going to turn the tables and let the world know who was boss. But now they knew better. They had been brought back down to earth with a thud. It was the thud of a cross as it was dropped into place by Roman soldiers. It was the thud of a great round stone as it was rolled into its place across the entrance of a tomb.

But, listen again. There are other sounds which rise above these deadening thuds. There are the excited voices of women, all striving to talk at once as they try to tell their friends about an empty tomb. There is the sound of running feet as Peter rushes to see for himself. There is the sound of a familiar voice calling from the lakeshore to men in a fishing boat saying, "Cast your net on the other side." There is the hushed voice of a doubting Thomas

exclaiming, "My Lord and my God!" There is the mighty
crescendo of a hallelujah chorus proclaiming the truth that
"the kingdoms of this world are become the Kingdom of
our Lord." (Revelations 11:15, KJV.) Here is the voice of
God Himself:

> He speaks, and listening to His voice,
> New life the dead receive;
> The mournful, broken hearts rejoice;
> The humble poor believe." [32]

Here is God's answer to those who see neither rhyme nor
reason to life. Here is His answer to those who accept the
verdict of the popular playwright when he concludes that
there is nothing but sorrow and meaninglessness at the
heart of existence. Here is His answer to those who believe
the scientist when he concludes that we are nothing but
"ship-wrecked passengers on a doomed planet." To them,
and to us, God is speaking through the mouth of the empty
tomb. He is saying, "Efforts to live the good life are not in
vain. The evil and self-seeking forces may mock at goodness and crucify love; but, the third day comes. There is
no evil powerful enough and no hate bitter enough to keep
the things of Christ in the grave. Truth crushed to earth
will rise again. It may be postponed, but not conquered;
deferred, but not defeated." It is not Pontius Pilate, but
Jesus Christ who has the last word. His is "the kingdom,
the power, and the glory, forever!" This was the affirmation added to "the Lord's Prayer" by persecuted disciples
in the first century. Surely, it can be our affirmation also.

Does this sound like escapism? Does this sound like
what the Communists call an "opiate of the people"? Contrary to popular belief, Easter is not an effort to make
men forget the evils of this world by pointing to the joys
of heaven. It is an effort to help men see how they can
rise above the evils of this world and become part of
God's plan for redeeming the world. The New Testament
keeps talking about God's concern for saving the world,
not for pulling men out of the world. It says, "God so
loved the world that He sent his only son to be a part of it
and to change it." And that son taught us to pray, "Thy

Kingdom come, Thy will be done *on earth.*" He prayed
(it states in John 17:15) that God would not take his disciples out of the world, but that He would send them into
the world to be his witnesses. No, Christians do not celebrate Easter primarily because the resurrection promises
a better life in the sweet by and by. We celebrate because
the resurrection promises that there is meaning and purpose in our efforts to live the good life here and now It is
significant that most of the poems in *Dr. Zhivago,* the
Pulitzer prize winning novel which was banned by the
Russian Communists, are about resurrection. Why did the
Communists ban that novel? Perhaps they see more
clearly than we do that the message of Easter is the most
earth-shaking word that has ever been spoken. They see
that it gives the lie to their crass doctrine of dialectical
materialism. They know that if the resurrection of Christ
is true, Communism and all that it stands for is false.

Several years ago I read somewhere the report of a
journalist from Moscow. He said that he listened to a
Communist lecturer attack the Christian faith for some
ninety minutes, proving to his own satisfaction that faith
in God was a dying surviver of capitalism. When he finished he invited discussion. A shy, timid, young man—a
typical village priest—stepped forward and asked permission to speak. "All right," the speaker said, "but not more
than five minutes." The young priest mounted the plat-
form and raising his hand in the traditional salute of the
Russian Church, he said, "Brothers and sisters, Christ is
risen!" Almost as one man, the audience made the response of their ancient church ritual, "He is risen indeed!"
Then, the young priest turned to the lecturer and said,
"I have finished. I have nothing more to say." What else
was there to say? He had proved his point. He had shown
that logic and lectures cannot destroy the fact of the living
Christ.

The New Testament reports that the Romans of the first
century referred to the Christians as "Those who have
turned the world upside down." (Acts 17:6, RSV.) Why
was this? As you read their semons in the book of Acts
or the letters of Paul, you find that the central theme of

all of them is the resurrection of Christ. What does that have to do with reform and revolution? How could the Romans say that this kind of preaching "turns the world upside down"?

Well, they evidently realized, even as the Communists do today, that once people become convinced that the way of force and the way of self-seeking do not have the final word, there is no way to keep them subservient and satisfied with injustice and inequality. If, as Jesus taught, it really is God's will that all men should live together as brothers, and that none should lord it over others, then no amount of force or false propaganda can keep them from striving for that way of life. Once men have seen and understood Christ, once they are convinced that he really represents God's will, once they are convinced that God did not leave him sealed in a tomb, then their ultimate loyalty will be to Him and to a society which recognizes the infinite worth of each person. They will be working that His Kingdom may come on earth as it is in heaven; and that, any way you look at it, means turning the world upside down. It may be that the Communists and other evil forces know this even better than we do. They know that if the story of the empty tomb is true, then their's is the lost cause. Their only hope is that Christian people will not really believe this story, will not believe it enough to start acting as if it were true.

But if we do accept the truth that is proclaimed by the empty tomb and by the suffering Christ on the Cross, then there is one more word that God can speak to us. It is a very personal word. It says, "You never walk alone." It is best symbolized by the two dejected disciples who were fleeing from Jerusalem toward Emmaus, after the crucifixion. As they walked, they were joined by one who talked with them about their disappointment, and who interpreted the Scriptures to them so they began to see that this was all a part of God's plan for the salvation of the world. Then, at the end of the journey, as they sat down to break bread together, and as he broke that bread with the gestures the Master alone used, they suddenly realized that their companion was Christ himself. From that moment on, they were never the same again. They rushed back to the city even though they knew they might be arrested and executed. They knew that God had not led them astray when they felt he was speaking to them through this carpenter of Nazareth. They knew that they could continue to walk with him to work with him in what he called "My Father's business." And, in a short time, as they began to compare notes with other disciples, they discovered that they were not the only ones who had had their personal experience with the risen Christ. There were some who had talked with him in the upper room where they had the Last Supper together. There were some who met him early one morning on the shore of the lake where he had first called them to be his disciples. There was even one, several years later, who insisted that he had met this same Christ on the road to Damascus. But all of them were unanimous in their testimony. As they listened to his words and as they responded to his presence, there came a power and a strength which they had never known before. There was a release from fear and a power to speak which lifted them out of themselves and made them feel like new persons. For instance, Peter, the man who had been afraid to stand up to the accusations of a serving maid, now stood before the Supreme Court of his nation, and even after they had had him thrown in prison and flogged, said, :"We must obey God rather than men." (Acts 5:29, RSV.)

There is only one possible explanation for this tremendous change in the lives of these disciples. It is the explanation which they themselves gave, and which no threat or torture could make them change. It was simply their conviction that their Master was still with them. This conviction created the Christian church. This conviction has kept the church alive. Explain it how you will. Interpret it in whatever words you choose. But the basic fact remains. The church was started, not to prove that Jesus Christ was alive. It started because men and women who had known Jesus best saw him alive. They became convinced that he was still with them and would continue to be with them if they were faithful to his teachings and his example.

Thus, it is the church which is God's ultimate answer to a skeptical world. Here truly is the "body of Christ" which no tomb can hold and no power can conquer. It is the vital, continuous, unbroken witness to the living hope which Peter was writing about in the first century. It offers a strengthening fellowship with the living Christ to those who will accept him and will join hands with other disciples in doing those things which Christ calls them to do. This was brought home to me most forcefully as I read Ernest Gordon's account of his experiences with the prisoners who built the infamous bridge over the river Kwai during World War II. He first describes how conditions went from bad to worse in that Japanese death camp. Civilized men became little more than animals, fighting each other for scraps of food, stealing from those who were dying, each man looking out only for himself. But then, something happened to make these men take a hard look at themselves. Angus McGillivray died of starvation. There was nothing new or startling about this. This happened every day. But what startled those who checked into his death was the discovery that he had deliberately gone without food himself in order to give his food to a friend who was dying. He saved the life of the friend, but became so weakened by his own lack of food that he died.

This story spread throughout the camp. And within a few days a group of Australian soldiers came to ask Ernest Gordon to lead them in a Bible study. They indicated that McGillivray's sacrificial death had made them start thinking that maybe there was something to Christianity after all.

Gordon tells how he started meeting with a small group of men to study the Bible by candlelight in a bamboo grove behind the latrine. He writes, "Through our readings and our discussions we came to know Jesus. He was one of us. He would understand our problems because they were the sort of problems he had faced himself. Like us, he often had no place to lay his head, no food for his belly, no friends in high places. He, too, had known bone-weariness from too much toil, the suffering, rejection and disappointments that are part of the fabric of life. . . . As we read and talked, he became flesh and blood. We saw him in the full dignity of manhood. He was a man we could understand and admire; the kind of friend we would like to have guarding our left flank; a leader we could follow." [33]

Soon the influence of these seeking Christian disciples started changing the whole atmosphere of that death camp. This idea that the purpose of life is to live for others inspired them to start planning ways they could help each other. Clean-up crews were organized to spruce up the hospital. Physical therapy teams were set-up to work with the disabled. Those who were prepared to teach skills or interesting subjects organized classes. Musicians scraped up some instruments and developed an orchestra which brought new beauty into their drab camp life. An engineer and a mechanic worked out a simple design for making an artificial leg; and started the amputees to work making new legs for themselves.

In short, there was new life in a death camp because men got to know Jesus Christ. Somehow, he broke through their bitter, hardened, cynical lives and called forth a response which Ernest Gordon calls "Miracle by the River Kwai." This is the response which always comes when men have a chance to know the real Christ. He does have the power to transform and change the lives of men.

He can change my life and your's if we are only willing to answer that persistent call, "Come, follow me!" If you will do this, "Easter will no longer be a story of strange things that happened to other people. It will become the wonderful thing that has happened to you. You will know that Christ lives, not because you have read it in a book, but because you have felt it in your heart and have found him by your side as you strugggled to live as he lived. You will know what Peter meant when he wrote: "We have been born anew to a living hope through the resurrection of Jesus Christ from the dead."

SUGGESTIONS FOR GROUP STUDY

As you have with the other sermons in this book, begin this session by examining the writer's ideas. The box on page 8 contains some suggestions for doing this.

Try this: Close your eyes and try to imagine life without hope. What do you see? Imagine life with no resurrection proving God's love for all. What do you see? Let several persons describe what they see through their imagination as they try to comprehend life without the hope the resurrection supplies.

Spend a part of this session in personal sharing. Describe experiences in which an awareness of God's love in the past has provided hope for a particular crisis. Describe experiences of God calling you into his future, your hope being the confidence that whatever that future entailed, God was there. And describe experiences of using hope as a resource as you face your day-to-day life.

This entire book of sermons is the writer's statement of faith, his testimony of his beliefs. You have studied it in order to come to a deeper understanding of your own faith and beliefs and in order to realize some ways in which you can put those beliefs into practice in your life.

Therefore, supply paper and pencils for each group member, and allow each person about one-third of this session time to write his or her own statement of beliefs. Each person will want to write a statement of what he or she believes about God, about Jesus Christ, about the Christian life, about suffering, about the moral law, about becoming a Christian, about the church, and about Christian hope as exemplified in the resurrection of Christ Jesus.

Allow time for several persons to read some or all of their statements, describing as they do so how this belief can or will affect their lives and their relationships to others.

Group members should retain their statements of belief, refer to them often, update them as they grow in understanding of their faith, and constantly seek new ways to incorporate their faith into their lives.

Conclude this session with sentence prayers of thanksgiving for each other, for God's revelation of himself, and for opportunities to grow together as Christians. Then form a circle, link arms, and pray together the Lord's Prayer.

FOOTNOTES

[1] From *A Rumor of Angels*, by Peter L. Berger, (Copyright © 1969 by Doubleday and Company) p. 120.

[2] From *Who Trusts in God: Musings on the Meaning of Providence*, by Albert C. Outler, (Copyright © 1968 by Oxford University Press) p. 77.

[3] From *A Rumor of Angels*, p. 112. Reprinted by permission.

[4] From *Science and the Modern World*, by Alfred N. Whitehead, (Copyright © 1925 by Macmillan Publishing Co., Inc., renewed 1953 by Evelyn Whitehead) p. 275. Reprinted by permission.

[5] From *A Rumor of Angels*, p. 121. Reprinted by permission.

[6] From *Who Trusts in God: Musings on the Meaning of Providence*, p. 75. Reprinted by permission.

[7] From *A Rumor of Angels*, p. 108.

[8] From *An Anthology of the Love of God*, by Evelyn Underhill, (Copyright © 1953 by McKay Publishing Company) p. 46. Reprinted by permission.

[9] From *Strength to Love*, by Martin Luther King, Jr., (Copyright © 1963 by Harper and Row Publishing Company) p. 141. Reprinted by permission.

[10] From *God's Image In Us*, by Edward N. West, (Copyright © 1960 by World Publishing Company) p. 5.

[11] From *A Future for the Historical Jesus*, by Leander Keck, (Copyright © 1971 by Abingdon Press) p. 35.

[12] From *The Man Christ Jesus*, by John Knox, (Copyright © 1941 by Willett, Clark and Company) p. 21.

[13] From *A Genuinely Human Existence*, by Stephen Neill, (Copyright © 1959 by Doubleday and Company) p. 49.

[14] From *Ibid.*, p. 50.

[15] From *The New Shape of American Religion*, by Martin E. Marty, (Copyright © 1959 by Harper and Row Publishing Company) p. 116.

[16] From "Orthodoxy" by G. K. Chesterton as quoted in *A Reader's Notebook*, by G. H. Kennedy. (Copyright © 1953 by Harper and Row Publishing Company) p. 170.

[17] From *The Grandeur and Misery of Man*, by David E.

Roberts, (Copyright © 1955 by Oxford University Press) p. 150.

[18] From *Jesus As They Remember Him*, by C. W. Quimby, (Copyright © 1941 by Abingdon Press) p. 132.

[19] From *The Stranger of Galilee*, by Reginald E. White, (Copyright © 1960 by Eerdmans Publishers) p. 95.

[20] From "Poll Points to a Paradox" in *The Christian Century* (September 15, 1965) p. 1118.

[21] From *Morality and Beyond*, by Paul Tillich, (Copyright © 1963 by Harper and Row Publishing Company) p. 24.

[22] From *The Spirit of Protestantism*, by Robert Brown, (Copyright © 1961 by Oxford University Press) p. 82. Reprinted by permission.

[23] From *Science Ponders Religion*, ed. by Harlow Shapley, (Copyright © 1960 by Appleton-Century-Crofts) p. 82. Reprinted by permission of Hawthorn Books, Inc. All rights reserved.

[24] From "God Speaks to a Godless World" in *The Christian Century* (May 25, 1966) by Mary Shideler, p. 676.

[25] From *Letters and Papers from Prison* (Revised Edition) by Dietrich Bonhoeffer, (Copyright © 1953, 1967, 1971 by SCM Press, Ltd.) pp. 121-122. Reprinted by permission.

[26] From *Who Trusts in God: Musings on the Meaning of Providence*, p. 107.

[27] From *A Footing on This Earth*, "Text," by Sara Hay, (Doubleday, 1966). Reprinted by permission of the author.

[28] From *Who Trusts in God: Musings on the Meaning of Providence*, pp. 105-106. Reprinted by permission.

[29] From *Life Together*, by Dietrich Bonhoeffer, (Copyright © 1954 by Harper and Brothers) p. 27-28. Reprinted by permission.

[30] From "Protean Man" in *Yale Alumni Magazine* by Dr. Robert Lifton pp. 14-21.

[31] From *Turning to God: A Study of Conversion in the Book of Acts and Today*, by William Barclay, (Copyright © 1964 by Westminster Press) p. 34.

[32] From "O For A Thousand Tongues" by Charles Wesley.

[33] From *Through the Valley of the Kwai*, by Ernest Gordon, (Copyright © 1962 by Harper and Brothers) pp. 137-138. Reprinted by permission.